MUGGLENET.com's
WHAT WILL HAPPEN IN
HARRY POTTER
7

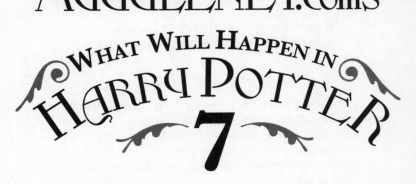

MUGGLENET.com's WHAT WILL HAPPEN IN HARRY POTTER 7

Who Lives, Who Dies, Who Falls in Love, and How Will the Adventure Finally End?

Ben Schoen, Emerson Spartz,
Andy Gordon, Gretchen Stull & Jamie Lawrence
with Laura Thompson

Ulysses Press

Dedicated to Harry Potter fans everwhere

ᔕ

The authors would like to thank the MuggleNet.com staff and
Quick-Quote-Quill.org for their help with this project.

Published in the United States by
Ulysses Press
P.O. Box 3440
Berkeley, CA 94703
www.ulyssespress.com

ISBN10: 1-56975-583-3
ISBN13: 978-1-56975-583-9
Library of Congress Control Number 2006907934

Acquisitions Editor: Nick Denton-Brown
Managing Editor: Claire Chun
Editors: Irene Elmer, Lily Chou
Editorial Associates: Elyce Petker, Rebekah Morris
Contributing Writers: Laura Thompson, Emily Ogle
Production: Matt Orendorff
Design: what!design @ whatweb.com

Printed in Canada by Webcom

4 6 8 10 9 7 5 3

Distributed by Publishers Group West

Table of Contents

Citation Key

AOL chat, 2000	America Online chat, AOL.com, October 19, 2000.
Barnes & Noble chat, 1999	Barnes & Noble chat online with J. K. Rowling, September 8, 1999.
Barnes & Noble chat, 2000	Barnes & Noble and Yahoo! chat online with J. K. Rowling, October 20, 2000.
Barnes & Noble interview, 1999	Barnes & Noble interview online, March 19, 1999.
BBC Christmas special, 2001	*Harry Potter and Me*. BBC Christmas special, December 28, 2001.
BBC Newsnight, 2003	"J. K.'s Order of the Phoenix Interview." BBC Newsnight, June 19, 2003.
Book Links, 1999	Judy O'Malley. "Talking with...J. K. Rowling." *Book Links*, July 1999.
Boston Globe, 1999	Stephanie Loer. "All about Harry Potter from Quidditch to the Future of the Sorting Hat." *The Boston Globe*, October 18, 1999.
cBBC Newsround, 2000	"J. K. Rowling talks about Book Four." cBBC Newsround, July 2000.
COS	J. K. Rowling. *Harry Potter and the Chamber of Secrets* (hardback). New York: Scholastic Press, 1998.
E! Online	E! Online News section, July 18, 2005.
Edinburgh Book Festival, 2004	Edinburgh Book Festival, August 15, 2004.
GOF	J. K. Rowling. *Harry Potter and the Goblet of Fire* (hardback). New York: Scholastic Press, 2000.
HBP	J. K. Rowling. *Harry Potter and the Half-Blood Prince* (hardback). New York: Arthur A. Levine Books, 2005.

ITV Report, 2005	Edinburgh Cubs press conference. ITV, July 16, 2005.
J.K.R. website	www.jkrowling.com
MuggleNet/TLC interview, 2005	"MuggleNet and The Leaky Cauldron interview Joanne Kathleen Rowling." July 16, 2005.
New York reading, 2006	"An Evening with Harry, Carrie and Garp." Radio City Music Hall, New York, August 1, 2006.
NPR Radio, 1999	National Press Club Author's Luncheon. NPR Radio, October 20, 1999.
OOTP	J. K. Rowling. *Harry Potter and the Order of the Phoenix* (hardback). New York: Scholastic Press, 2003.
People, 1999	"J. K. Rowling: The 25 Most Intriguing People Of '99." *People* magazine, December 31, 1999.
POA	J. K. Rowling. *Harry Potter and the Prisoner of Azkaban* (hardback). New York: Scholastic Press, 1999.
Richard and Judy interview, 2006	*The Richard and Judy Show* with Richard Madeley and Judy Finnigan, Channel Four Corporation (U.K.), June 26, 2006.
SS	J. K. Rowling. *Harry Potter and the Sorcerer's Stone* (hardback). New York: Scholastic Press, 1997.
Time, 2000	"Essay: A Conversation with J. K. Rowling; A Good Scare." *Time* magazine, October 30, 2000.
WBUR Radio, 1999	*The Connection* with Christopher Lydon, WBUR Radio, October 12, 1999.
World Book Day, 2004	World Book Day chat with J. K. Rowling, March 4, 2004.

Foreword

I'm going to go out on a limb and say that you're reading this for one of two reasons. A) You're a MuggleNet fan who has been anticipating this book for some time now, or B) You picked up this book at a bookstore because it looked interesting. If it's the latter, you might be wondering, What the heck is MuggleNet.com, and who cares what they think is going to happen in Harry Potter 7?

Like the cover says, MuggleNet.com is the #1 Harry Potter website, receiving over 20 million hits per month. I founded the site at the age of 12 in the fall of 1999 as a bored homeschooler with too much free time on my hands. For the first few years of the site's existence, I flew solo as captain and first mate. Now I manage a volunteer staff of over 120 dedicated and passionate Harry Potter fans of all ages from around the globe, all of whom take pride in working for the site. The "Mighty MuggleNet" (as J.K.R. herself calls it) is truly a labor of love. It consists of hundreds and hundreds of pages of information, discussion, movie clips, newspaper articles, radio interviews, and more— anything you can possibly imagine that relates to Harry Potter. It's a lot of work, but we love what we do. We get to organize events that draw tens of thousands of fans, set up interviews and live chats with movie stars, cover and attend glitzy, star-studded movie premieres and conventions, make sponsored visits to the movie sets, and even interview J. K. Rowling! And, oh yeah, write books.

Warning! If you're looking for Top Secret information about what's going to happen in Book 7, this isn't the place. We can tell you how we *think* things will unfold, but we don't know for sure— nobody does, except J. K. herself. J. K. (or "Jo," as she asks us to call her whenever we chat) sometimes makes us privy to the inside scoop, but on Book 7 she's keeping extremely quiet.

So why should you read this book? Simply, because our *job* is to follow Harry Potter—the latest news, the hottest theories. We've heard just about every crackpot theory fans have dreamed up, and we know just about everything J.K.R. has ever said loud enough for a reporter to hear. We're walking HP encyclopedias—as close to being "experts" as you can get.

People will be picking up Harry Potter books for generations to come, but we are the lucky few who can say, "We were there." We will remember the crazy, late-night madness of book releases and the teeming crowds of fans all over the world gathering in honor of Harry Potter. We will remember watching a book about a boy wizard seduce millions of kids away from their TV sets. We will remember spending countless hours arguing with our friends about Snape's loyalties and whether Harry would survive the series. And, with so many burning questions yet to be answered, we will certainly remember debating about how this great adventure will finally end in the seventh and last book of the Harry Potter series.

Most fans want Book 7 in their hands right *now*, and believe me, we feel your pain. We've waited impatiently for every single book, but now that the end is almost near… I can't stress enough how important it is to savor these moments of anticipation and speculation, because these moments will provide us with memories that we will fondly cherish in the future. It's been said that anticipation of a thing is often better than the thing itself. Of course, we're not saying that this book will be better than the actual Book 7 in any way; but we do hope it will whet your appetite for Book 7 and provide you with a way to cope while you wait for the final installment of Harry's adventures.

—Emerson Spartz
founder of MuggleNet.com

Book 7 Basics

What Will the Title of Book 7 Be?

No official title has been released yet, so on this question we can only speculate. Eagle-eyed fans, however, will have noticed that on two separate occasions Warner Brothers has patented possible titles—none of which have been declared the real thing.

Pick any possible combination of "Harry Potter and the some-thing-something" and you'll find that it has probably already been patented: Harry Potter and the Alchemist's Cell, Harry Potter and the Battle for Hogwarts, Harry Potter and the Chariots of Light, Harry Potter and the Final Revelation, Harry Potter and the Green Flame Torch, Harry Potter and the Hallows of Hogwarts, Harry Potter and the Hogsmeade Tomb. You can see the logic behind some of them: "Harry Potter and the Green Flame Torch" would have been a fine working title for Book 4, *The Goblet of Fire*. But "Harry Potter and the Great Revelation"? Are you kidding us? Maybe these have been patented for merchandise, possibly trading card games, or perhaps Warner Brothers is just trying to throw us off the scent.

We believe the official title has not yet been declared for several reasons. Most significantly, J. K. Rowling is a writer who constantly rethinks and revises her work. In September 2006, she announced that she'd decided on the Book 7 title...until she was taking a shower that morning and an even better title popped into her head! [New York reading, 2006] Furthermore, since Book 7 is such an important one, J.K.R. will not want to release the title until closer to publication time in order to build maximum hype for the book's release. Finally, releasing the title would commit her to it. If the title reveals a specific plot clue that she subsequently wants to change, she will have no choice but to write it in or change the title. This is especially true for Book 7, where we imagine she is constantly revising the finer details in order to get them just right.

So when *will* we learn the title of Book 7? We're not sure. However, in the past, J.K.R. has announced the titles of her upcoming books about one year in advance. She'll probably stick to a similar timeline for Book 7. But be prepared for a few tricks in between: Remember the *Pillar of Storgé* incident where a fan posing as J.K.R. released a fake title, only to have the real J.K.R. come out to squash the rumor by announcing the true title?

How Long Will Book 7 Be?

In September 2006, the *Daily Mirror*—a U.K. tabloid—reported that J.K.R. had written 750 pages and was only *halfway* through writing. J.K.R. later refuted the claim [J.K.R. website, Rubbish Bin section], however, and we'll certainly take her word over that of some gossip rag. Besides, there's simply no way the book would be 1,500 pages long. J.K.R. has already said she thinks that Book 7 will be shorter than *Order of the Phoenix* (though she's wouldn't guarantee it) [ITV Report, 2005]. But assuming the book *will* be shorter than OOTP, which weighed in at a whopping 870 pages, she's still given herself room to write a respectable 869-page tome. And with all the loose ends she needs to wrap up, don't be surprised if Book 7 comes in close to that length. After all, there are no more books for her to fix errors or include information she wished she had included before. So she will be checking this book twenty times over to make sure that she has included all the necessary information and filled any remaining holes.

When Will Book 7 Finally Hit the Shelves?

Ah, the big question that everyone wants an answer to. At Muggle Net.com, we get e-mails asking this question everyday.

Only J.K.R. and her publisher know the exact release date of Book 7. And they're not telling. If this information somehow got leaked, heads would roll. So for now, "mum" is the word. There are a few telling clues, however, that allow us to speculate on when we'll see Book 7 in the stores. One popular theory is that the book will be released on July 7, 2007, or 07/07/07. Seven is the most powerful and magical number in the Harry Potter series, after all, and Harry himself was born at the end of July, the seventh month. The last three Potter books have all been released on Saturdays (in order to allow eager young fans to attend midnight releases the night before), and 07/07/07 conveniently happens to fall upon, you guessed it, a Saturday. Furthermore, all six previous Potter books have had their world premiere in the U.K. in either June or July. (The American release dates were slightly later for a couple of the earlier books. But once Harry Potter got HUGE in the U.S., the U.K. and American release dates were aligned in order to keep overly zealous Potterites from smuggling British copies into the U.S. and spoiling the plot for American readers.) It certainly seems like all the stars have aligned for July 7, 2007.

But despite all the clues pointing us to a 07/07/07 release, we find this publication date highly unlikely. Why? Because the *Harry Potter and the Order of the Phoenix* movie will be released on July 13, 2007. The Harry Potter films are big business for Warner Brothers and J. K. Rowling. Fans around the globe will be anticipating the release with sheer excitement, and Warner Bros and J.K.R. won't want to divert that excitement for either the movie or the book by pitting one against the other. They'll want to focus all the hype on just one Harry Potter product at a time. So say goodbye to the 07/07/07 theory.

The earliest release date we think is possible for Book 7 will be late 2007 or early 2008. A summer 2008 release looks more likely still for a couple of reasons. J.K.R. revealed in September 2006 that she "wasn't even close to finishing" the book [J.K.R. website, Rubbish Bin section]. That means she still has much to write and finalize (and there is lots to be wrapped up). And even after she finishes writing, she still has to send the book to her publishers for editing, promotion, and Americanizing (because the British and American editions are released simultaneously), all of which can take the best part of six months to a year. Furthermore, every previous Harry Potter book has seen its world premiere in either June or July, and every previous Harry Potter book has been enormously successful. So if it ain't broke, why fix it? And since summer 2007 is out of the question because of the *Order of the Phoenix* movie, then summer 2008 seems like the clear choice.

But we should note once again, like everything in this book, these are merely educated predictions. Only J.K.R. knows the true answers to these questions and she is closely guarding all of her secrets. On a recent flight back from New York, increased airport security meant there was a risk that she would be parted from her manuscript. J.K.R. wouldn't be parted from it, however, and after much pleading, security allowed her to take it on. She mentioned that if they hadn't let her board with it, she would have probably jumped on a boat and sailed the entire way back to England [J.K.R. website, News section]. So rest assured, fellow Potterites, even though everything about Book 7 is hush-hush, the manuscript safely remains in very good hands.

The Story So Far

Let's face it: It's been a *long* journey. No one could have guessed, when *Harry Potter and the Sorcerer's Stone* was published in 1997, that we would still be waiting on tenterhooks for the next book in the series a decade later. J. K. Rowling, who has climbed gracefully into the ranks of great authors, continues to write books that excite and enthrall us long after they have been returned to the shelf. Our own book is primarily concerned with looking forward at what will be, but it seems prudent to step back first and remind ourselves why we are still here.

The idea for Harry Potter came to J. K. Rowling in 1990 when she was on a delayed train from Manchester to London. She had not brought a pen with her, and she was too shy to ask anybody to lend her one, so she simply sat back and let Harry and his world enter her head. She notes on her website that "if I had had to slow down my ideas so that I could capture them on paper I might have stifled some of them." If she is reading this today, we think we speak for Harry Potter fans worldwide when we thank her sincerely for leaving that pen at home.

That same evening, J.K.R. began pouring her ideas onto paper. Over the next six years, she wrote, rewrote, and edited what was going to be the first of seven Harry Potter books. Finally, in 1996, she handed her completed manuscript to her first agent, who rejected it out of hand. The second agent she tried, Christopher Little, recognized the potential immediately and contacted Bloomsbury, a British publisher.

The rest, as they say, is history. In June 1997, *Harry Potter and the Sorcerer's Stone* tumbled into bookstores worldwide. Many of us were introduced to it indirectly, by friends who swore on their lives it was the best book that they'd ever read. Somewhere, somehow, we read it. We got hooked. Harry Potter became our caffeine, became the reason we read. Across the world, thousands of parents rejoiced as they saw their children genuinely interested in reading for the first time.

But let's be fair: What's *not* to like about it? A boy wizard who attends a magical school, fights trolls, plays sport on broomsticks, learns how to brew potions, meets a three-headed dog, and triumphs over the most feared Dark wizard of all time. It's a story that leaves nothing, yet everything, to the imagination, saturating the senses with imagery while leaving the mind free to explore it all at will. Breathtaking in its originality, it was a harbinger of things to come. Just over a year later, we got our next Potter fix.

Harry Potter and the Chamber of Secrets was published in July 1998. This time, we entered the bookstore with a clear purpose in mind. We had met the characters; now we wanted to see them develop. We wanted to know more about the history of Harry and his world. This was, of course, exactly what we got. We learned more about Lord Voldemort's past and Harry's abilities, and we met new and exciting characters.

Harry Potter and the Prisoner of Azkaban appeared in July 1999. Many people have told us that this remains their favorite book, and it's very easy to see why. In it, we were introduced to the tortured soul of Sirius Black, a character dear to many hearts. We also met Remus Lupin, another firm favorite. Azkaban appeared for the first time, as did its spooky guardians, the Dementors.

Harry Potter and the Goblet of Fire was published in July 2000. Bigger than the first three books put together, it marked a turning point in the Potter series, both in terms of content and in terms of its unprecedented worldwide popularity. Although the books had been turning progressively darker, we had not before witnessed what we all dreaded: the death of a good character. In Book 4, Cedric Diggory was murdered before our eyes. This taught us that the Harry Potter world is magical but not Utopian. "It is my belief," said Dumbledore at the end, "...that we are all facing dark and difficult times" [GOF, pp. 723-24]. His words were grimly prophetic; if we finished the fourth book having learned one thing, it was that Lord Voldemort had definitely returned.

A painful three-year hiatus ensued, while we were left with burning questions as to what was happening in Harry's world. Finally, on June 21, 2003, *Harry Potter and the Order of the Phoenix* hit bookstores. Its release was met with worldwide euphoria, with book parties from New York to New Zealand, from Los Angeles to London. Once again, with the murder of Sirius Black, we experienced death firsthand. Perhaps most significantly, we also saw the truly evil nature of the Dark Side. We witnessed the first major battle between members of the Order of the Phoenix and the Death Eaters down in the depths of the Ministry of Magic. We saw corruption at the highest level. If we thought *Harry Potter and the Goblet of Fire* was dark—well, we hadn't seen anything yet.

Harry Potter and the Half-Blood Prince, the penultimate book in the series, was released in July 2005 and quickly became the fastest-selling book in history. Borders reported sales of over one million books in the first 48 hours [E! Online, 2005]. One thing was clear from reading the book: the magical world was now totally at war. And with Dumbledore apparently dead, the safety Harry had once enjoyed at Hogwarts had vanished. Harry's world fell down around him as he battled Voldemort both physically and mentally. At the end of the book he felt alone, distanced from his friends, about to face a new challenge: finding the remaining Horcruxes and destroying the very evil that had shadowed his life for so many years.

And there we have it. Six books down, one to go. It's important to remember, however, that we were not all there from the beginning. Some fans picked up the series much later than others did, perhaps starting with a Christmas present from their parents. Others read *Harry Potter and the Goblet of Fire*, wondering what all the hype was about, but were seen back in the bookstore four hours later buying the first, second, and third books with almost unholy enthusiasm.

Whatever drew us into Harry Potter, we are now united as fans. And as fans, we now feel the great uncertainty in the series as a whole. The battle between good and evil has begun. But lest we forget, this is no fairytale. There will be, and have been, losses on both sides, and we cannot sit back and cheerfully assume that the forces of good will win. Yet while we are uncertain as to the outcome of the war, we still cannot wait to get our hands on the final book. We are as eager now as we were the first time we read *Sorcerer's Stone*.

Why are we still so enthralled? First and foremost, because we have come so far. We began by sharing in the wild adventures of a young boy wizard and now we are empathizing with a grief-stricken adolescent as he attempts to conquer evil once and for all. We have seen Harry grow, develop, and mature and form relationships and bonds. How can we not want to know what happens next?

There are also the subtle and clever parallels to the real world. We see Harry coping with the difficulty of fitting in at a new school, the pressure of having to prove himself, having to deal with loss. Is there a reader out there who has not, at some point, experienced Harry's plight? On the other hand, the books offer a way out of the real world: a place to forget your own problems, troubles, and tribulations.

Finally, the books have united us as fans. To us, you are either a Harry Potter fan or you aren't. We don't care about religion, race, or color, only about what you think will be the outcome of the war, which girls Harry has taken a liking to, what you think Voldemort is up to at this very second. Those outside the fandom don't understand it, but we fans really feel a sense of belonging when we line up at the bookstore at 2 a.m. sharing the latest theories and ideas or simply screaming Harry's name to bewildered passersby, awaiting the release of the next book in the series.

It's impossible to talk about "The Story So Far" without mentioning the internet. A behemoth that now spans thousands of websites, hundreds of forums, and hundreds of thousands of fans, the internet is the main channel we use to get our Potter fix in between book releases, be it with fan fiction, fan art, or good old-fashioned theory discussion. It is the only place where you can chat about Harry Potter to your heart's content with fans who are as passionate as you are.

And let's not forget the Harry Potter movies. They represent a huge part of worldwide "Pottermania." Each movie has a character of its own, sometimes mirroring the character of the books and sometimes taking on a whole new perspective. The movies offer fresh new angles, particularly with the personal spin that is put on them by the frequent rotation of directors.

So that's the story so far. Harry Potter has now spanned sixteen years, six books, and three hundred million copies, yet we think we speak for each and every fan when we say that we are still aching for more. There is no doubt in our minds that Book 7 will be the most explosive, the most exciting, and the most entrancing book of the series. While we race to the release, we are asking ourselves the same question that we have been asking for the best part of a decade: "What will happen next?"

From all of us here at MuggleNet.com, we hope we have done this question justice.

Enjoy the book.

What J.K.R. Says

J. K. Rowling has kept particularly quiet about Book 7. But she has occasionally presents us with snippets of information that give us a taste of what is to come. Here's an overview of what she has said.

Quick Facts

To many readers' dismay, there will be no Quidditch matches in Book 7 [MuggleNet/TLC interview, 2005]. There will be entirely too much else going on. In fact, J.K.R. has even said that Quidditch matches have been the "bane of [her] life in the Harry Potter books" [MuggleNet/TLC interview, 2005]. So don't expect to see any snitch-catching in the final installment.

The last word in Book 7 is "scar" [People, 1999].

All characters (except Voldemort) are redeemable [New York reading, 2006]. Don't be shocked if Draco Malfoy joins the good side.

We'll Be Seeing More of...

RITA SKEETER   This buzzing journalist just won't go away. She's been a useful and clever spy in the past, and it's likely that Harry and his friends will find a use for her again [Edinburgh Book Festival, 2004].

VIKTOR KRUM   The Bulgarian Quidditch player isn't out of the picture yet [World Book Day, 2004].

DOLORES UMBRIDGE   Umbridge stirred up quite a fuss in Book 5. She's back in Book 7 to cause more commotion [MuggleNet/TLC interview, 2005]

THE FORD ANGLIA   The Ford Anglia saved Harry and Ron from the giant spiders in Book 2. Perhaps the old car will save them again in Book 7 [Barnes & Noble chat, 1999].

THE SORTING HAT   The Sorting Hat always has a helpful message for the students at the beginning of the year. This final year will be no different. And perhaps the Sorting Hat is more significant than we think. As J.K.R. has said, "There is more to the Sorting Hat than what you have read about in the first three books. Readers will find out what the Sorting Hat becomes as they get to future books" [Boston Globe, 1999].

Since we haven't learned anything major about the Sorting Hat yet, the big secret must be revealed in Book 7.

TWO-WAY MIRROR   Before Sirius Black dies in Book 5, he gives Harry one of a pair of two-way mirrors that can be used for communication. After Sirius dies, Harry smashes his mirror. The mirror might return in Book 7. Perhaps Harry will get to say good-bye to Sirius after all [World Book Day, 2004].

We'll Learn More about Dumbledore ...

Albus Dumbledore was the greatest wizard of his time. How did he get to be who he was? In Book 7, Dumbledore's family is likely to play a significant role:

> ***Emerson Spartz:*** *Dumbledore is unrivaled in his knowledge of magic —*
>
> ***J.K.R.:*** *Mmhm.*
>
> ***ES:*** *Where did he learn it all?*
>
> ***J.K.R.:*** *I see him primarily as someone who would be self-taught. However, he in his time had access to superb teachers at Hogwarts, so he was educated in the same way that every-one else is educated. Dumbledore's family would be a profitable line of inquiry, more profitable than sweet wrappers.*
>
> ***Melissa Anelli:*** *His family?*
>
> ***J.K.R.:*** *Family, yes.*
>
> ***MA:*** *Should we talk about that a little more?*
>
> ***J.K.R.:*** *No. But you can! [Laughter.]*

Dumbledore had a wealth of information that could be very useful to Harry. It's worth counting on something in Dumbledore's past playing a key role in Book 7. As to what it will be, your guess is as good as ours.

And what about Dumbledore's "gleam of triumph"? In Book 4, when Harry is describing Voldemort's rebirth, he says that Volde-mort used his (Harry's) blood to re-create his own body. When he says this, he sees a gleam of triumph in Dumbledore's eyes [GOF, p. 696]. J.K.R. has said many times that this fact will be very important to Book 7:

> ***MA:*** *Does the gleam of triumph still have yet to make an appearance?*
>
> ***J.K.R.:*** *That's still enormously significant. And let's face it, I haven't told you that much is enormously significant, so you can let your imaginations run free there.* [MuggleNet/TLC interview, 2005]

Why is this gleam of triumph so important? You'll have to read Book 7 to find out for sure.

... and Lily Evans

We were supposed to learn something important about Harry's mother in Book 5, and we're going to learn something even more important in Book 7, something pivotal to what Harry has to do:

> *"Now the important thing about Harry's mother, the really, really significant thing, you're going to find out in two parts. You'll find out a lot more about her in Book 5, or you'll find out something very significant about her in Book 5, then you'll find out something incredibly important about her in Book 7. But I can't tell you what those things are, so I'm sorry, but yes, you will find out more about her because both of them are very important in what Harry ends up having to do."* [WBUR Radio, 1999]

Finally, J.K.R. has said that in Book 7, we will learn the significance of Harry's eyes: "Harry has his father and mother's good looks. But he has his mother's eyes and that's very important in a future book" [Boston Globe, 1999]. We think the significance of his eyes has something to do with their color—they are green, like Lily's eyes. As to what that means, we are not entirely sure.

Love and Romance

The hormones were raging in Book 6. We've been onto Ron and Hermione since Book 4 (most of us, anyway), but *Half-Blood Prince* sealed the deal. J.K.R. alluded to this during a Q&A session with fans:

> *Nina: I just wanted to know what Hermione would see if she looked into the Mirror of Erised?*
>
> *J.K. Rowling: Well—(crowd laughs and applauds)—at the moment, as you know, Harry, Ron, and Hermione have just*

finished their penultimate year at Hogwarts and Hermione and Ron have told Harry that they're going to go with him wherever he goes next. So at the moment I think that Hermione would see most likely the three of them alive and unscathed and Voldemort finished.

But I think that Hermione would also see herself closely entwined with...another...person (crowd roars and applauds loudly). I think you can probably guess. Thank you, very good question. I've never been asked that before. Now we have another. [New York reading, 2006]

J.K.R. hasn't said much about the Harry/Ginny relationship, or about the other romances in the series (Lupin and Tonks, Draco and Pansy). But she has said that Book 6 should have "made the trends clear" in terms of what to expect when it comes to romance [MuggleNet/TLC interview, 2005].

Based on that hint, we say that love will conquer all.

How Will Book 7 Unfold?

If Harry wants to kill Voldemort, J.K.R. says that he must take Dumbledore's advice and destroy the Horcruxes:

MA: Here at the end you sort of get the feeling that we know what Harry's setting out to do, but can this really be the entire throughline of the rest of the story?

J.K.R.: It's not all of it. Obviously it's not all of it, but still, that is the way to kill Voldemort. That's not to say it won't be extremely torturous and winding journey, but that's what he's got to do. Harry now knows—well he believes he knows— what he's facing. Dumbledore's guesses are never very far wide of the mark. I don't want to give too much away here, but Dumbledore says, "There are four out there, you've got to get rid of four, and then you go for Voldemort." So that's where he is, and that's what he's got to do.

ES: It's a tall order.

J.K.R.: It's a huge order. But Dumbledore has given him some pretty valuable clues and Harry, also, in the course of previ-

ous six books has amassed more knowledge than he realizes. That's all I am going to say.

Destroying all of the Horcruxes will prove to be quite a challenge, but it is what Harry's has to do to succeed. So that is what we expect him to do in Book 7. As to whether he will survive, J.K.R. is leaving us to speculate. After all that he's been through, we think it's fair that he survives.

Who Lives, Who Dies

J.K.R. wrote the final chapter of Book 7 over a decade ago [Book Links, 1999]. Recently, she says she changed that chapter slightly. One character who was originally slated for death got a reprieve, while two others who weren't going to die now will [Richard and Judy interview, 2006]. And back in 2001, she said, speaking of that same final chapter, "This is really where I wrap everything up. It's the Epilogue, and I basically say what happens to everyone after they leave school—those who survive, because there are deaths, more deaths, coming" [BBC Christmas special, 2001].

We've seen throughout the first six books that J.K.R. does not hesitate to kill off characters close to Harry. As she says, "We are dealing with pure evil! So they don't target the extras, do they? They go straight for the main characters... Or I do" [Richard and Judy interview, 2006]. This makes it seem likely that more than one of our beloved characters will get the axe in Book 7.

Will Harry, Ron, and Hermione make it out alive? We think so. In 1999, J.K.R. did a reading at the Barnes & Noble bookstore in Naperville, Illinois. While her appearance is undocumented, MuggleNet webmaster Emerson Spartz had a chance to speak with the manager about the event. According to her, during the question-and-answer session with the fans, J.K.R. was asked if Harry, Ron, and Hermione live through Book 7. Surprisingly enough, she answered the question and said yes. It's important to keep in mind that this happened before everything that J.K.R. said was documented, and before the books had become international bestsellers.

The three main characters are going to be in the line of fire a lot during the many upcoming battles between good and evil. So there's a strong chance that not all three characters will survive. We wouldn't go placing death bets on Ron just yet, however. In an interview conducted in 2000, J.K.R. said, "Mostly they are really worried about Ron. As if I'm going to kill Harry's best friend" [Time, 2000].

It's worth keeping a watchful eye on Hermione, though: "What I find interesting," J.K.R. said in the same interview, "is [that] only once has anyone said to me, 'Don't kill Hermione,' and that was after a reading when I said no one's ever worried about her. Another kid said, 'Yeah, well, she's bound to get through OK.' They see her as someone who is not vulnerable, but I see her as someone who does have quite a lot of vulnerability in her personality." Hermione is a complex character and her vulnerabilities may cause her problems. Let's just hope Hermione makes it through unscathed.

So that leaves Harry. Here J.K.R. has given us the runaround many times. Many people have encouraged J.K.R. to write more than seven books. Recently, J.K.R. said that it will be impossible for anyone else to write a sequel to Book 7. What better way to prevent it than to kill off Harry?

> *"I can completely understand the mentality of an author who thinks I'm going to kill him off because then there can be no non-author-written sequels, so they call it. So, it will end with me. And, after I'm dead and gone, they won't be able to bring back the character."* [Richard and Judy interview, 2006]

Agatha Christie killed off Poirot; why can't J.K.R. do it with Harry? (Don't do it, J. K., please!) We're hoping she just keeps throwing around the idea of Harry dying to keep us all on our toes, and that she's really planning to allow Harry to live happily ever after.

J.K.R. hasn't revealed who is going to die and who is going to live. But, as we mentioned before, she has said that there are "deaths, more deaths, coming." So don't get too attached to any-body in the Potter series because J.K.R. has already proven that she has no qualms killing off some of our most beloved characters.

But whatever fate J.K.R. chooses for our heroes and heroines, we're sure that she won't disappoint us with the last Harry Potter novel. Soon all of the teasing and question dodging will come to an end. J.K.R. will answer all of our burning questions with the release of Book 7, and the boy wizard who has captivated a generation of young people will realize his destiny at last. But for now, enjoy the ride as we come down the home stretch!

Dumbledore

Of all the questions raised by the events of *Half-Blood Prince*, the question of Dumbledore's fate is perhaps the one that is most widely debated. A vast army of fans believe that Dumbledore is actually alive and well, that his death was all an elaborate hoax. However, a number of clues suggest just the opposite. Let's explore the arguments here.

Dumbledore Is Dead

What is there to be said about Albus Dumbledore? He is a great and powerful wizard, a benevolent Headmaster, a tireless fighter in the war against Voldemort, and a lover of socks. Albus Dumbledore is a great man. He might also be very well dead.

Harry believes beyond a shadow of a doubt that Snape killed Dumbledore in cold blood, because he saw him do it with his own two eyes. Although Harry doesn't want to believe that Dumbledore is dead, he has to, because he saw what happened. As readers, however, we have learned not to take things at face value. Harry is convinced that he saw Dumbledore die after Snape cast the Killing Curse, but then again, an entire street full of Muggles were convinced that they saw Sirius Black kill Peter Pettigrew.

Clearly, what people think they see doesn't count for much in the world of Harry Potter, but there is plenty of magical evidence to prove what really happened. Everything, from the last spell Dumbledore cast, to the behavior of Fawkes the phoenix, to the nature of the Headmaster's office itself, intimates that Dumbledore is no more.

Harry Immobilized

The evidence starts with Harry. The most important thing is not what Harry sees as Dumbledore is hit with the Killing Curse, but what Harry experiences. Before his confrontation with Draco, Dumbledore paralyzes Harry, placing him in a Full Body-Bind. This spell renders Harry immobile, forced to watch the action taking place from the safety of his Invisibility Cloak, but unable to intervene. However, as Snape's curse hits its mark and Dumbledore's body falls to the ground, Harry discovers that he can move again [HBP, p. 597]. For some reason, the spell that Dumbledore placed on him is lifted. Harry's experience earlier that year, when Draco Malfoy cast the same spell on him on the Hogwarts Express, shows us that an immobilized person cannot be released from the Full Body-Bind until the spell is lifted [HBP, pp. 153-56]. Tonks did the honors on that occasion, but no one lifts the spell from Harry this time. This suggests that the spell was lifted for another reason. Harry acknowledges that other reason not long afterward:

> *He had known there was no hope from the moment that the*
> *full Body-Bind Curse Dumbledore had placed upon him*
> *lifted, known that it could have happened only because its*
> *caster was dead.* [HBP, p. 608]

FOR THE LOVE OF SOCKS

Sometimes, it's the little things in life that matter. Socks, for instance. Who would have thought something so trivial could be so important? And yet, socks are mentioned time and again in the Harry Potter series. Harry removes spiders from his socks, Mrs. Weasley spends time washing socks, a cleverly placed sock sets Dobby free, and even Dumbledore expresses a great love of this most common of foot apparel [SS, p. 19; GOF, p. 155; COS, p. 338; SS, p. 214].

Dumbledore professes a love of socks in the very first book in the series, *Harry Potter and the Sorcerer's Stone*. During the Christmas holidays, Harry discovers the Mirror of Erised, a magical mirror that shows "nothing more or less than the deepest, most desperate desire of our hearts" [SS, p. 213]. In the mirror, Harry sees his family, Ron sees himself standing alone as the best of his brothers, and Dumbledore, well, Dumbledore has a rather peculiar answer as to what he sees when he looks in the mirror:

> *[Harry says] "What do you see when you look in the mirror?"*
> *"I? I see myself holding a pair of thick, woolen socks....*
> *One can never have enough socks," said Dumbledore.*
> *"Another Christmas has come and gone and I didn't get a*
> *single pair. People will insist on giving me books."* [SS, p. 214]

If Dumbledore is being truthful, and, considering his rather odd answers to so many questions, it is entirely possible he is, it would seem that the Headmaster has a great fondness for a garment many put little to no thought into whatsoever. Why is this? There is no one answer. Perhaps he uses socks as a metaphor for something much greater, or perhaps he means nothing more than the common, everyday object with which we are all acquainted. Despite being one of (if not the) most powerful wizard of the age, Dumbledore is a man of simple pleasures. You can't get much simpler than a lovely pair of thick, woolen socks. Perhaps Dobby isn't the greatest sock lover of all.

No one lifts Dumbledore's spell from Harry, so the only way Harry could be released is for the spell to have been rendered useless—in short, for the person who cast the spell to have died. If Dumbledore had been alive, Harry would have remained frozen; the spell would not have relinquished its hold until someone magically removed it. Dumbledore's death is what would allow Harry to regain control of his body. While Harry's perception can be skewed, the laws of magic cannot be broken, and they provide the first hard piece of evidence that Dumbledore is dead.

The Body

After regaining his mobility, Harry pursues Snape into the castle grounds. It is here, while returning to the castle, that Harry discovers Dumbledore's body lying in a crumpled heap, in front of a group of shocked, confused students. Dumbledore is lying "spread-eagled [and] broken" [HBP, p. 608]. His arms and legs are sticking out at strange angles, his eyes are closed, and a trickle of blood is running down the corner of his mouth [HBP, pp. 608-609]. The message given is plain: Dumbledore is dead.

Many people argue (or hope) that Dumbledore faked his death in order to work behind the scenes and trick Voldemort into a false sense of security. This seems plausible enough, and a great wizard like Dumbledore likely could have pulled this off. But if Dumbledore had chosen to fake his death, he likely wouldn't have chosen to do it like this.

Dumbledore loves his students deeply and he knows that they are living in dangerous times. Voldemort is extremely dangerous, and there's no guarantee that Dumbledore would succeed in bringing him down even if Dumbledore were working undercover. Therefore, Dumbledore would probably have faked his death in a more valiant manner than the one he "chose," a manner that would have inspired his followers to continue the fight with passion. Instead, he was killed in the most sickening and demoralizing way: by his trusted friend, Severus Snape. And what could be less inspiring to his students and to the rest of the wizarding world than to die by apparent treachery? It's doubtful that Dumbledore, who loves his students so deeply that he wished to be buried near them at Hogwarts [HBP, p. 629], would willfully leave his students crushed like this.

The Song of the Phoenix

When Harry tells the crowd in the hospital wing that Dumbledore is dead, they react with varying degrees of horror and disbelief. Not long afterward, Fawkes begins to sing "a stricken lament of terrible beauty" around the Hogwarts grounds [HBP, p. 614-15]. The phoenix's song seems to echo the grief that everyone is feeling, and it provides another magical clue. As Dumbledore told Harry long before, phoenixes make "highly *faithful* pets" [COS, p. 207], remaining ever loyal to their owner. Fawkes is a constant presence in Dumbledore's office, but when Dumbledore is hit with the Killing Curse, the phoenix abandons his perch to circle the grounds and sing a woeful tribute to his master. Phoenixes are intelligent, powerfully magical creatures, and if Dumbledore had only been feigning death, it seems unlikely that Fawkes would have reacted as he did. Fawkes, who is so loyal that he can sense his master's movements and desires, would have known that Dumbledore was not dead, so he would have no reason to sing his "stricken lament."

Much later that evening, when Harry goes back to his dormitory, he notices that Fawkes has stopped singing and the grounds have gone silent:

> *And he knew, without knowing how he knew it, that the*
> *phoenix had gone, had left Hogwarts for good, just as*
> *Dumbledore had left the school, had left the world...* [HBP, p. 632]

This is another clue that suggests Dumbledore is dead. Fawkes would not leave Hogwarts without Dumbledore. If Dumbledore were faking his death, he would certainly return to Hogwarts again at some point; he cares too much for the school and students not to do so. For Fawkes to leave Hogwarts for good means that Dumbledore, too, has gone to a place from which he cannot return.

Dumbledore's Office

The office which Dumbledore inhabited for so many years provides another clue that he has died. When Harry agrees to talk with

McGonagall shortly after Dumbledore is killed, he is surprised to notice that they are heading not to McGonagall's office, but to Dumbledore's. It dawns on him slowly that McGonagall, who served the school as Deputy Headmistress for so long, became Headmistress the moment Dumbledore died, "so the room behind the gargoyle was now hers" [HBP, p. 625]. More important than Harry's realization is the fact that the office automatically accepts her. The Head's office is enchanted and allows only those who rightfully belong there to enter. We know this because the previous year, when Dolores Umbridge ousted Dumbledore and appointed herself Head, the office magically sealed itself and barred her from entering [OOTP, p. 625]. McGonagall, however, is allowed to enter at will: The room is acknowledging that Dumbledore is dead. This is probably the same type of magic that has caused Dumbledore's portrait to appear on the wall.

Harry notices it as soon as he enters the office [HBP, p. 626]. Apparently the school is charmed to sense when a change of power has taken place and hangs the portrait of the newly deceased Headmaster or Headmistress on the wall so that the portrait can act as an advisor to the new Head. According to former Headmaster Armando Dippet, or more specifically, Dippet's portrait, the portraits in the Head's office are "honor-bound to give service to the present Headmaster of Hogwarts" [OOTP, p. 473]. For a portrait of Dumbledore to have joined the ranks of the other deceased former Heads means that the room recognizes that Dumbledore's time as Headmaster is over, and that he has passed away.

The Funeral

Finally, there is the funeral itself to consider. This is the only glimpse of a wizarding funeral that we are given in the books, but based on the characters' reactions, it seems that several elements are unusual, even for funerals of the magical variety. Foremost among these is the appearance of the white marble tomb, which is met with several screams [HBP, p. 645].

We don't see anyone cast the spell to make the tomb appear; the magic seems to happen naturally and to the surprise of many of the onlookers. Dumbledore, who had once told McGonagall that he wished to be "laid to rest here, at Hogwarts" [HBP, p. 629], may well have put the magic in place long ago. Whether he did so or not, the fact remains that white flames encompass Dumbledore's body, and that they give way to a white marble tomb. This would not have happened if Dumbledore had been faking his death. The marble tomb and the way it magically materializes provide further proof that Dumbledore has died. Harry recognizes it, Fawkes recognizes it, the school itself recognizes it, and the very tomb that forms around Dumbledore's body recognizes it. Dumbledore is dead.

Dark Magic

Despite all the evidence that seems to affirm Dumbledore's death, some people stoutly maintain that Dumbledore is alive.

One of their strongest arguments seems to be that even magical objects can be fooled by someone with a great deal of power. The curse on Harry, the Head's office, the portrait, Fawkes, and the white tomb could all have been tricked into behaving as though Dumbledore were dead when he is really alive. It's a decent theory. After all, the Goblet of Fire was tricked into giving up four names instead of the normal three [GOF, pp. 270-71]. Why couldn't these other objects have been fooled, especially by a wizard as powerful as Dumbledore?

The answer to this question can be found over and over again in the series. While it is possible to hoodwink objects like the Goblet, it takes powerful Dark magic to do so [GOF, p. 279]. Although Dumbledore has the power to wield that kind of magic, he does not use it. In the series, Dumbledore stresses the importance of choice over ability, saying, "It is our choices…that show what we truly are, far more than our abilities" [COS, p. 333], and Dumbledore has chosen not to use his abilities to their full potential if it means succumbing to the Dark Arts.

Dumbledore is strong enough to use any type of magic he sees fit to use. What makes him different from power-hungry wizards like Voldemort is the fact that he will not use Dark magic simply because he can—and that's the whole point. While Dumbledore could easily have faked his own death and fooled all the magical objects into behaving as though he were truly gone, he could only have done so by using a form of magic that he is not willing to use. The magic is working of its own accord, behaving as though Dumbledore is dead.

Dumbledore Is Alive

If Dumbledore died, surely the Order of the Phoenix would crumble, and with it the fight against evil. Without Dumbledore, surely Harry would be helpless in his lone crusade against his enemy. If Dumbledore died, then surely Voldemort would start to do whatever he liked (and we all know that wouldn't be pretty).

For Dumbledore to fake his own death and leave the world in the lurch would be unthinkable. And yet, a lot of evidence suggests this is what he's done.

It's true that J.K.R. herself has said the following: "I see that I need to be a little more explicit... and say that Dumbledore is definitely dead" [New York reading, 2006]. This can hardly be good news for fans of the "Dumbledore is alive" argument. But there is so much evidence to contradict this statement that we might not want to take what she says here at face value. After all, would J.K.R. really think it was a good idea to destroy the second-largest post-HBP mystery in a single stroke? It would be very strange indeed if she did. So let's look at the evidence from the books instead.

The facts in the books suggest that Dumbledore is alive. What's more, they also show that the faking of his death is no conspiracy, cooked up by the Order. The expression on Snape's face as he delivers the Avada Kedavra curse to Dumbledore hints at that [HBP,

p. 595]. Snape's Killing Curse is real, and if Dumbledore finds some ingenious way of getting around it, he is acting alone.

Snape, McGonagall, Potter, Lupin—all believe that Dumbledore is dead. But he might not be.

The Big Moment

One single moment might be proof that Dumbledore faked his own death:

> *Harry's body became instantly rigid and immobile, and he felt himself fall back against the tower wall, propped like an unsteady statue, unable to move or speak.* [HBP, p. 584]

This piece of action happens at the moment when Draco bursts through the door onto the ramparts and casts Expelliarmus at Dumbledore. It seems like such a small gesture on Dumbledore's part—immobilizing Harry under his Invisibility Cloak to keep him safe—but it may be much more than that. Dumbledore may want to make sure that there will be a witness to tell the world that he has been killed.

Following the supposed killing, Harry runs after Snape and eventually catches him [HBP, p. 602]. He starts hurling curses at Snape like confetti, but not one hits the mark: Snape blocks the lot, mostly before they are half out of Harry's mouth. Is anybody suggesting, even for a second, that Dumbledore wouldn't have been capable of blocking curses just as easily? He was certainly quick enough to cast an incantation-free (and quite probably wandless) Petrificus Totalus on Harry, even if he had just drunk a bellyful of emerald potion. Why doesn't he just block Draco's curse and swat him aside like the annoying little brat that he is?

The answer seems to be this: He needs Draco there because he wants to fake his own death. He needs Draco to try to kill him, and indeed to believe he *has* killed him, so he can secretly avoid the curse and then disappear. And he needs Harry there because he needs a witness.

A Pleasant Chat

Dumbledore probably feels a mixture of disappointment and relief when he realizes that Draco doesn't have the guts to kill him. Sure, he wants his plan to go ahead, but at the same time perhaps he hopes that Draco will turn out all right after all. Draco's inability to cast his final curse suggests that this may actually be the case. Anyway, Dumbledore and Draco end up having a lengthy chat, during which Dumbledore doesn't make the slightest effort to escape.

Dumbledore knows by now that Draco is not going to pull the trigger. If he were just trying to stay alive it's the ideal time to get away. After all, the Death Eaters are fighting down below, and it can only be a matter of time before reinforcements arrive on the ramparts. But secretly, this may be just what Dumbledore is waiting for. His plan is simply to keep Draco talking until someone arrives who will (attempt to) kill him properly.

He even takes the opportunity to test Draco, telling him (quite inaccurately) that he can't possibly defend himself without a wand: "I have no wand at the moment.... I cannot defend myself" [HBP, p. 586].

The truth is that he could have trussed up Draco like a Christmas turkey before Draco knew what was happening, even without a wand. Wizards less accomplished than Dumbledore use wandless magic all the time; Snape once cast a wandless Accio at the Shrieking Shack to summon some ropes he'd just used to tie up Remus Lupin [POA, p. 360]. It would be foolish to suggest that Dumbledore couldn't manage a wandless Incarcerous, or perhaps a repeat performance of Petrificus Totalus.

But he doesn't. He just plays for time, waiting for someone to come along who will finish the job that Draco has bungled.

A Not-So-Pleasant Chat

But it's not just one person who comes along—it's four: Amycus and his sister Alecto, a Death Eater with a brutal-looking face, and Fenrir Greyback. The new arrivals greet the sight of Draco and a wandless Dumbledore with vicious glee.

> *"Dumbledore cornered!" he said, and he turned to a stocky*
> *little woman who looked as though she could be his sister and*
> *who was grinning eagerly. "Dumbledore wandless, Dumble-*
> *dore alone! Well done, Draco, well done!"* [HBP, p. 592]

Dumbledore's response is to go right on talking, as though he were welcoming them to a tea party. His casual, easygoing manner when he's talking to Draco is understandable; he knows that Draco isn't going to kill him. You could hardly say that about the new arrivals, though; they are absolutely itching to finish him off. Dumbledore doesn't fear death, of course, but surely he wouldn't be so jovial if he didn't have a plan up his sleeve. Even if he weren't afraid for himself, he would be extremely anxious about what was going to happen to Harry, to the Order, to anyone who was on his side, after he died. No man who cared so much about defeating Voldemort could be so relaxed if he thought that the Dark Lord was about to celebrate his most important murder ever.

But Dumbledore is relaxed. He makes pleasant conversation, and he remembers his manners at all times even with Greyback oozing revoltingness at him.

> *"Good evening, Amycus," said Dumbledore calmly... "And*
> *you've brought Alecto too.... Charming... "* [HBP, p. 593]

Why so calm and pleasant? Possibly because he has a plan up his sleeve ready to go.

Fawkes

The phoenix is a remarkable bird, and Fawkes is remarkable even for a phoenix. He's always there when he is needed; he saves Harry in the Chamber of Secrets [COS, p. 322], and he even takes an Avada Kedavra for Dumbledore in the battle at the Ministry of Magic [OOTP, p. 815]. His tears can heal the most terrible wounds; his song has the power to calm whoever hears it even if they are suffering terrible torment, as shown by the lament he sung after Dumbledore "died" [HBP, pp. 614-15]. But on this night, the night when he is most needed, we're supposed to believe that he doesn't bother to show up.

Perhaps he is sulking. Perhaps Dumbledore has given him the day off. Or perhaps he knows that his master is in no danger and that he isn't needed. Which choice sounds the most convincing?

There are so many ways that Fawkes could have helped if he were needed. His tears could have cured Dumbledore of the effects of the emerald potion; he could have taken the Avada Kedavra for his master; he could have plucked Dumbledore from the rooftops and carried him to safety. He can even Apparate with Dumbledore when he wants to [OOTP, p. 622], and so even if Dumbledore was too weak to cast spells anymore, Fawkes could have taken him away anywhere, in an instant. On top of that, he can communicate with Dumbledore; he always knows what Dumbledore is thinking [OOTP, p. 470].

But he wasn't there: he was snuggled up in Dumbledore's office instead, enjoying a bit of a rest. This most likely wouldn't have happened if Dumbledore's death had been real.

THE DEPARTURE OF FAWKES

Fawkes shares a remarkable bond with Dumbledore that allows him to communicate with him just as effectively as talking. Indeed, Dumbledore does talk to him when he asks Fawkes to go and watch for Dolores Umbridge and warn him if she is around [OOTP, p. 470], and Fawkes understands. It is likely that Dumbledore was only saying the words out of habit, however, and that Fawkes understood without them. After all, when Harry was in the Chamber of Secrets, Fawkes felt Harry's loyalty to Dumbledore even from that distance (and without words) and brought him the Sword of Gryffindor to help him fight the basilisk [COS, p. 320]. It should therefore come as little surprise to find out that with his master gone, Fawkes too will not return. As Harry realized when the phoenix finished his lament after Dumbledore's death:

> *"And he knew, without knowing how he knew it, that the phoenix had gone, had left Hogwarts for good..."*
> [HBP, p. 632]

The Killing Curse

Did anybody notice what happens to Dumbledore when Snape's Avada Kedavra hits him in the chest?

> ...*Dumbledore was blasted into the air. For a split second he seemed to hang suspended beneath the shining skull, and then he fell slowly backward, like a great rag doll, over the battlements and out of sight.* [HBP, p. 596]

But Avada Kedavra doesn't do that!

Every time this curse has been used in the series, it's had the same effect. There is a flash of blinding green light and a loud rushing sound, and the victim simply crumples to the floor, unmarked. That's what happens to the Riddle family [GOF, p. 4], to Frank Bryce [GOF, p. 15], to Cedric Diggory [GOF, p. 638]. Each and every one just crumples to the ground, without a scratch on him.

When Snape casts his spell at Dumbledore, the green light is there, and even though there is no mention of a rushing sound, it could have been covered by Harry's scream. But what happens next is probably not Avada Kedavra. Dumbledore is flung over the battlements as though he has been hit by Relashio or an exceptionally strong Expelliarmus. Why doesn't he just fall to the floor?

Why? Possibly because he modified the curse or got out of its path before it hit him. Avada Kedavra is famously unblockable [GOF, p. 216], but Dumbledore did a number of miraculous things with magic as he dueled with Voldemort in the battle at the Department of Mysteries [OOTP, pp. 813-14]. There's no reason he couldn't pull something out of the bag here, too, even without his wand. And why does he set it up so that he's thrown from the ramparts? Because he needs to be alone when he "dies." He needs to make sure that nobody witnesses the moment of impact so that he can create a mocked-up dead body with a spot of Transfiguration, and get out as fast as he can. For that, he is willing to sacrifice a bit of realism and

The incantation "Avada Kedavra" is a corruption of the well-known magical phrase "abracadabra," which is used by children and entertainers to indicate that they are doing magic. Abracadabra itself has an interesting history, as it was used as a healing spell in early European cultures to drive disease from the body of a patient. Its likely source is either the Arabic *abra kadabra* (meaning "may the things be destroyed"), or the Aramaic *abhadda kedhabhra* (meaning "disappear with these words").

hope that in the heat of the moment, nobody notices. And nobody does. Not one person, even Snape, believes that he is still alive.

The Locket

So on to the final piece of evidence: the open locket.

Dumbledore has been careful up to this point, and he's done a pretty good job. He has even remembered to remove the Body-Bind Curse from Harry, so that Harry can tell everyone that he is dead. He has plenty of time to knock together a convincing corpse and get out of the way.

There is one thing that he hadn't planned on, though, one thing that had never even crossed his mind. The Horcrux is a fake. Dumbledore knows that Harry needs to find all the Horcruxes if he is going to defeat Voldemort. So it is vital that he knows that this one isn't real.

He has only one option. He has to set up the scene so that Harry cannot fail to find the locket and read the note inside. It's a risk, of course, but one that he has to take. In the cold light of day, for us readers, it's pretty obvious: the locket just *happens* to drop out of dead Dumbledore's pocket onto the ground beside him, and open conveniently with R.A.B.'s note sticking out? Not likely.

But Harry finds the locket in the heat of the moment, in shock, and in that situation it's very hard to be logical. Dumbledore's risk pays off: Harry doesn't suspect a thing.

In fact, nobody suspects a thing. Dumbledore leaves a trail of clues so wide that he might just as well put a sign on the door saying, "Don't worry. I'm not dead really." But he gets away clean with it. The Death Eaters think he is dead. The Order thinks he is dead. Harry thinks he is dead.

The only question that remains is, why would Dumbledore want them to think it?

Dumbledore's Reasons

Nobody is suggesting that Dumbledore is secretly a baddie, or that he is faking his death so that once Voldemort has gone he can reappear and take his place. So why would he pretend to be dead?

As usual, he has his reasons.

Dumbledore has probably realized that the only way to defeat Voldemort is to work unseen. Really unseen. Unseen and alone. Voldemort knows him, Voldemort will work around him, and Voldemort will find ways to stay out of his way if he knows where Dumbledore is. But with Dumbledore gone, apparently dead, Voldemort will drop his guard.

In Book 7, assuming Dumbledore is alive, yet invisible and unknown, he will fight against the Dark Lord in ways he could never do if Voldemort knew he was alive. Voldemort won't even know who is attacking him, or from where. In Book 7, Dumbledore will be the invisible destroyer.

But to make this strategy work, Dumbledore will have to be totally alone. Nobody, not even his closest friends, can know the truth, because if the secret gets out, the game will be up. Dumbledore has upset a lot of people by pretending to be dead, but he will be prepared to live with the results of that for the sake of the cause. When Voldemort lies dead at last, it will all have been worth it.

The Verdict

If we were looking at just the evidence presented in the books, we'd side with the "Dumbledore is alive" theory. However, J.K.R. herself says that Dumbledore is dead ("definitely dead," to be precise).

And she has never publicly lied about Harry Potter. She has been evasive, yes, but never a liar. So until we catch her in the act, we will just have to take her word on this issue. J.K.R. is the creator of the story, and of Dumbledore himself, and she is not to be argued with. Dumbledore is dead.

His death is a truly a tragedy. He was a great man, a powerful wizard, and an irreplaceable asset in the fight against Voldemort. Dumbledore was one-of-a-kind, and it's understandable that readers want to look for some sign proving that his supposed death is just a hoax. Yet just because his loss is hard to cope with does not make it any less true. We will probably see Dumbledore, or rather his likeness, again in the series, but only through his portrait that now hangs in the Headmaster's office. While this portrait has the ability to speak and advise, it is not Dumbledore. Dumbledore, as we know him, is gone.

As Dumbledore once said so long ago, "After all, to the well-organized mind, death is but the next great adventure" [SS, p. 297].

Dumbledore did not fear death. He spent his life in the pursuit of good, leaving a lasting impression on all who knew him. It's time to accept that his time has come to an end, and time for readers to let Dumbledore rest in peace.

Neville's Destiny

Neville Longbottom is a fascinating character. In the series, we've seen him go from playing the role of bumbling comic relief (in his inept attempts to memorize and cast spells) to that of a brave and formidable wizard (when he accompanies Harry to the big show-down at the Department of Mysteries in OOTP and joins the battle when Death Eaters enter Hogwarts in HBP). But through it all, there has always been an intriguing aura of mystery surrounding Neville. Why does Trelawney's prophecy parallel Neville as well as Harry? Why is his memory so suspiciously poor? Why were Neville's parents tortured to the point of insanity, and how did they thrice defeat Voldemort?

In OOTP, an emotional new subplot developed as Neville came face to face with Bellatrix Lestrange, the despicable Death Eater who led the torture of his parents. As we head into the final book, everyone wants to see the ultimate showdown between Neville and Bellatrix. Neville wants his vengeance, and we want him to get it.

The Importance of the Prophecy

At this point, everyone knows that Trelawney's prophecy could have applied to either Neville or Harry. After all, both boys were born at the end of the seventh month to parents who had thrice defeated Voldemort and survived [OOTP, p. 842]. Voldemort's attack on Harry at Godric's Hollow, however, marked Harry as the chosen one, giving Harry the scar and its special ability to see into Voldemort's mind. If Voldemort had chosen Neville instead of Harry that night so long ago, Neville would have been marked, and we all would have been reading about Neville Longbottom, the Boy Who Lived, for the last ten years.

Many readers have concluded that the shared nature of this prophecy has marked Neville for a destiny interwoven with Harry's. J.K.R. has said that this is not the case, however [J.K.R. website, F.A.Q. section]. Neville's history has been set up to show the true nature of prophecies, that there is a measure of free will and choice within any prophecy. We see evidence of this when Voldemort *chooses* Harry at Godric's Hollow (for more on prophecies see Chapter 13). But in no way does this mean that Neville is an unimportant character. In fact, we think there is still much to be revealed about the boy who could have been the Chosen One.

Why Is Neville So Forgetful?

One thing that has never quite made sense about Neville is his magical ability, or apparent lack thereof, in the first few books of the series. Neville is a pure-blood wizard, but for most of the series, can't cast an accurate spell or make an effective potion to save his life. Even Neville admits his lack of magical talent, saying, "...everyone knows I'm almost a Squib" [COS, p. 185].

Why is the pure-blood son of two talented Aurors so very inept at magic? Well, for starters, everyone's magical ability is different. Just as it is possible for two Muggles to produce a magical child, it is possible for two pure-bloods to produce a Squib, a child with no magical ability whatsoever. This could be the case with Neville, but there may be another possibility.

In the first book, Neville is sent a Remembrall [SS, p. 145], a magical memory device that glows red if the person holding it has forgotten something [SS, p. 145]. At first, it does not seem significant that poor, forgetful Neville has such a device sent to him. Indeed, it glows scarlet the very first time he holds it [SS, p. 145]. At second glance, though, there may be more to Neville's Remembrall than originally meets the eye.

Although we see Neville's Remembrall turn red, indicating that he has forgotten something, we never learn what it is that Neville has forgotten. Perhaps it is something as meaningless as a homework assignment. Or perhaps Neville has forgotten something of extreme importance. Remember, J.K.R. loves to drop seemingly inconsequential hints that come back to play important roles in later books. This is the case with the Brazilian boa constrictor that in SS foreshadows Harry's ability to speak Parseltongue [pp. 27-28], as well as Polyjuice Potion, seemingly introduced for laughs in COS when Hermione is turned into a large cat-human hybrid [pp. 225-26], but is vital to the plot of GOF. The theory here is that maybe Neville has had his memory modified for some reason, a reason we think may have something to do with Neville's parents.

Little is known about Neville's parents. Our main knowledge of them is that they were tortured to the point of insanity by Bellatrix Lestrange and the Death Eaters after Voldemort's original fall from power [GOF, pp. 602-603]. They have been residing in St. Mungo's ever since. We know that Neville was born around the same time as Harry [OOTP, p. 842], and that Harry, though just a year old when his parents were murdered, can recall certain things about that fateful night [POA, pp. 239-40]. Neville was even older when his parents were tortured, and if he was with them when it happened, it is reasonable to think that he would be able to recall these events as well. It's possible that Neville could have witnessed something that night that someone didn't want him to remember.

This has two implications: First, Neville's memory could have been modified to keep him from remembering something important that either his parents or the Death Eaters said or did that night. This is unlikely because Neville was so young he wouldn't have understood what was happening even if he did witness it. Also, if the Death Eaters were really concerned about what he was seeing, they could have just killed him. The other possibility is that someone cast a Memory Charm on Neville, not to erase anything in particular that he may have witnessed, but to purge the overarching memory of his parents' torture. If this is the case, it is probable that the person was not ill-intentioned in casting a Memory Charm, but instead wanted to save a young child from the horrid images of watching his parents suffer. But owing to Neville's continued forgetfulness, this mysterious person may have made the memory charm a bit too strong. We've seen this happen before in the series, when Barty Crouch Sr. put a strong Memory Charm on Bertha Jorkins, accidentally causing permanent damage [GOF, p. 685].

If Neville is under a strong Memory Charm, it would certainly explain why he has so many problems learning and retaining information and practicing magic. This is just a theory, though, and does not account for the fact that, in the later books, Neville's magical skills begin to develop rapidly. Neville's early lack of skill may be nothing more than the result of meager self-confidence. Nevertheless, the possibility of deliberate tampering with Neville's memory remains.

Neville vs. Bellatrix

While Harry has never known his parents, Neville has grown up visiting two parents who don't know *him*. We all know why Neville has been forced to suffer this terrible fate: The Death Eaters, most notably Bellatrix Lestrange, tortured Neville's parents until they went permanently insane, when poor Neville was just a baby.

Neville is no longer a baby, however. In fact, he's growing into a supremely capable wizard. After Neville hears about ten Death Eaters' escaping from Azkaban, including three responsible for the torture of his parents, he throws himself headlong into Dumbledore's Army and begins practicing magic like mad. The subsequent change in Neville is significant. Harry can't help but notice that Neville "was improving so fast it was quite unnerving" [OOTP, p. 553]. Motivated by the desire to protect his friends and avenge his parents' torture, he rapidly improves.

All of this spells bad news for Bellatrix and good news for fans who want to see Bellatrix get her comeuppance. Neville, with a broken nose, meets Bellatrix for the first time in the Department of Mysteries at the end of OOTP and the mutual hatred between the two is evident:

> *"Longbottom?" repeated Bellatrix, and a truly evil smile lit her gaunt face. "Why, I have had the pleasure of meeting your parents, boy...."*
>
> *"I DOE YOU HAB!" roared Neville, and he fought so hard against his captor's encircling grip that the Death Eater shouted, "Someone Stun him!"* [OOTP, p. 800]

Bellatrix's sickening taunt, followed by Neville's roar of hatred, shows that this fight has become personal. You can bet that in the seventh and final book, with the ultimate battle between good and evil sure to occur, these two will have ample opportunity to settle the score once and for all. And because of the depth of their hatred for one another, neither will be happy until the other is dead.

We're confident that when the dust from this battle clears, Neville will emerge victorious. He will win because not only is he driven by revenge, but he's also driven by the power of love. He deeply loves his parents as well as his friends. Motivated by this love, he will improve his magical abilities even more than he did in HBP. When that happens, Bellatrix will be no match for Neville. Just as the power of love will give Harry the edge he needs to defeat the Dark Lord, the power of love will allow Neville to rise up and defeat his arch nemesis as well.

Draco's Destiny

From the moment readers first glimpse young Draco Malfoy standing in Madam Malkin's Robes shop, it becomes apparent that he will play an active role in the Harry Potter series. Haughty, selfish, and heartlessly cruel, Draco is a thorn in Harry's side from the moment they meet, never missing an opportunity to harm or harass the Boy Who Lived and his friends.

In the first five books of the series, Draco is every bit the pampered prince of the Malfoy family. Doted upon and spoiled beyond reason, he is little more than a carbon copy of his father, Lucius Malfoy. Although Lucius plays the role of the upstanding aristocrat in wizarding society, he is devoted to the Dark Arts, despises Muggles and Muggleborns, and is obsessed with the so-called purity of blood. Lucius is a faithful follower of Lord Voldemort, and he instills in Draco all of his own twisted beliefs. Draco accepts his father's viewpoints without question, parroting Lucius's thoughts and actions.

His dogmatic devotion to his father's way of thinking leads young Draco to join the ranks of the Death Eaters, and this is when we see a change in Draco.

Death Eater or Rebel: Does He Have a Choice?

The Draco we see at the end of *Half-Blood Prince* is far different from the arrogant young boy we had come to know in the earlier books. The spoiled young wizard with the world at his fingertips has become a frightened young man, in far over his head, with few choices left and even fewer places to turn for help.

At the beginning of *Half-Blood Prince*, Draco is just as boastful as always, reveling in his new status as a Death Eater. His boasting quickly dies away, however, when he realizes the seriousness of what Lord Voldemort has asked him to do. With each failed attempt on Dumbledore's life, Draco becomes more frightened and desperate. By the time he begins searching out Moaning Myrtle's company for sympathy and solace, Draco's devotion to the Dark Lord has wavered to the point that Voldemort has started using fear against him as a motivator. Voldemort has threatened to kill the entire Malfoy family if Draco does not somehow manage to murder Dumbledore. Even so, when Draco finally gets the opportunity to face Dumbledore, who is wandless and injured, he is unable to carry out Voldemort's orders. Draco does not kill Dumbledore, even to save his own life and the lives of his parents. By the end of the book, Draco does not have many options and he knows it:

> *"I haven't got any options!" said Malfoy, and he was suddenly white as Dumbledore. "I've got to do it [kill Dumbledore]! [Voldemort'll] kill me! He'll kill my whole family!"* [HBP, p. 591]

Draco is correct in believing that Voldemort will not hesitate to kill his whole family, but he is wrong about his options. Draco has options and he has a choice to make: Will he remain a Death Eater or will he rebel?

After Dumbledore's death, Draco would seem to have four different options from which to choose:

- He can leave the Death Eaters and seek refuge with the Order of the Phoenix, falling under the protection that Dumbledore has offered him and his family.
- He can follow in Severus Snape's footsteps and become a spy for the Order, feigning allegiance to Voldemort while leaking information to Voldemort's enemies.
- He can defect from the ranks of the Death Eaters and go into hiding on his own.
- He can remain a faithful Death Eater and follow Voldemort to the bitter end.

Of these four options, all but one seems almost entirely implausible.

Will He Seek Refuge with the Order?

It is unlikely that Draco will trade his role as a Death Eater for the safety that the Order can offer him and his family. In addition to being a bigot, Draco is very proud. He and Harry have been enemies from the moment they met. Draco has done nothing but mock the Weasleys for their poverty and condemn Hermione for being Muggleborn. No matter how desperate Draco's situation may be, he will not allow himself to ask for help from the very people he has set himself so staunchly against.

There is another reason why Draco will not seek refuge with the Order. Evidence suggests that he does not believe that the Order can really protect him from Voldemort:

> "...I can help you, Draco."
>
> "No, you can't," said Malfoy, his wand shaking very badly indeed. "Nobody can." [HBP, p. 591]

He had said much the same thing to Moaning Myrtle earlier that year. Myrtle had offered to help him, and Draco had tearfully refused her, saying, "No one can help me" [HBP, p. 522]. It is unclear why Draco is so certain that the Order cannot help him. It is likely, however, that in adopting his father's bias concerning all witches and wizards not of pureblood descent, Draco really believes the Order is inferior to the Death Eaters because it is made up of so many half-bloods, Muggleborns, and people he considers to be blood traitors. It is also likely that Draco's fear of Voldemort has caused him to become irrational, terrified to seek out the help he so desperately needs.

Draco believes wholeheartedly that no one, not even Dumbledore and the Order, can help him out of the situation he's gotten himself into. In his confrontation with Dumbledore, Draco does experience a brief moment of uncertainty, lowering his wand ever so slightly as he considers Dumbledore's offer. That uncertainty dies along with Dumbledore. Many witches and wizards believed that Dumbledore was the most powerful wizard of the age. If Dumbledore, with all his power, could not escape Voldemort's wrath, Draco has to believe that he doesn't stand a chance. The Order could not save Dumbledore, and Draco will not ask the Order to protect him.

In addition, there appears to be a third factor keeping Draco from seeking refuge with the Order. If Draco goes to the Order for help, Voldemort will take his anger with Draco out on his parents, Lucius and Narcissa. Voldemort can be just as cruel to his followers as he is to his enemies. He will not hesitate to kill the Malfoys and Draco knows it. Although Dumbledore offered to extend the Order's protection to Narcissa and Lucius as well, Draco knows that his parents will not accept the Order's help. They have been Voldemort's servants for far too long. Also, if Draco does not believe that the Order can protect him from Voldemort, why would he believe it can protect his family?

Draco will not seek refuge with the Order. His immense pride is only one factor stopping him. His belief that the Order cannot protect him, coupled with his fear concerning what Voldemort will do to his parents if he goes into hiding with the Order, are also keeping him from seeking out the Order's protection.

Will He Turn Spy for the Order?

Likewise, Draco will not turn spy for the Order. If there is one thing we know about Draco Malfoy, it's that he is a coward. Draco likes to talk boastfully and feign fearlessness. He loves to get under people's skin, hurting and bullying them, but only when he knows he is protected in some way. Usually, Draco makes sure that he is under the protection of a teacher, or that Crabbe and Goyle are there to back him up. When Draco is on his own, he is not nearly so cocky. He doesn't have the guts to follow through on his threats; he would sooner run from danger than stand and face it. The six books are filled with examples of Draco's cowardice:

Draco "let out a terrible scream and bolted" when encountering the cloaked figure in the Forbidden Forest [SS, p. 256].

He lay on the ground screaming, "I'm dying....It's killed me!" when Buckbeak slashed at his arm during Care of Magical Creatures [POA, p. 118].

According to Fred Weasley, Draco "nearly wet himself" with fear when he encountered a Dementor on the Hogwarts Express [POA, p. 97].

Vain and weak, Draco doesn't have what it takes to be a spy. As Snape has proven, to be a spy takes courage. It takes cunning. It means not being afraid to carry out orders, no matter what those orders may be. To be a spy is to lead a dangerous life, living in constant jeopardy. If Draco is unwilling to go to the Order for help, he will certainly not go to the Order offering his own help and services. Ill-equipped as Draco is to be a Death Eater, he has nowhere near the amount of courage he would need to betray the Death Eaters and join in the fight against Voldemort.

Even if he were willing to be a spy, Draco lacks the ability. He is still a young wizard, unskilled in many of the more difficult forms of magic that a spy would find necessary. Shortly before his death, Dumbledore tells Draco:

> *"...I suspected you.... [but] I did not dare speak to you of the mission with which I knew you had been entrusted, in case he used Legilimency against you."* [HBP, p. 591]

Snape has been successful as a spy because he is an accomplished Legilimens who can block others from accessing his thoughts. We know from a conversation Draco had with Snape that Draco studied this type of magic briefly:

> *"...Aunt Bellatrix has been teaching you Occlumency, I see. What thoughts are you trying to conceal from your master, Draco?"*
>
> *"I'm not trying to conceal anything from* him, *I just don't want* you *butting in!"* [HBP, p. 322]

While Draco may be studying Occlumency, it is safe to assume that he is not yet an expert in this particular branch of magic, certainly not as skilled as Voldemort or even Snape. If he were to turn spy for the Order, Voldemort would know it within a matter of moments, and Draco would be killed—or worse, used to deceive, and ultimately to destroy, the Order.

For various reasons, Draco will not go to the Order, neither to gain their protection nor to offer them his services as a spy. This leaves two options open to Draco. He can remain faithful to Voldemort and the Death Eaters, or he can leave the Death Eaters and go into hiding.

Will He Remain Faithful to Voldemort?

Out of fear, Draco may remain faithful to Voldemort for a short while, but he lacks the courage and conviction it takes to be a truly devoted follower. Draco joined Voldemort for his father's reasons, not his own. This is why he will never be a true asset to the Dark Lord.

Draco himself may not realize this. He may think that he truly espouses his father's beliefs. Draco has probably never questioned his pureblood upbringing, never questioned the lessons he was taught as a child. But as he quickly learns, talking about exterminating Mudbloods and actually raising a wand to cast a Killing Curse are two different things. Pampered little Draco is no more a killer than Dudley Dursley. A bully, yes, but not a killer.

At age eleven, Draco tells Harry, "You'll soon find out some wizarding families are much better than others, Potter. You don't want to go making friends with the wrong sort....You hang around with riffraff like the Weasleys and that Hagrid, and it'll rub off on you" [SS, pp. 108-109]. A year later, discussing the Chamber of Secrets, he comments, "I'm quite surprised the Mudbloods haven't all packed their bags by now....Bet you five Galleons the next one dies. Pity it wasn't Granger" [COS, p. 267]. And again, after Cedric Diggory's murder, he taunts Harry, saying, "You've picked the losing side, Potter! I warned you!...Too late now, Potter! They'll be the first to go, now the Dark Lord's back! Mudbloods and Muggle-lovers first!" [GOF, p. 729]. These are not the words of a child. Draco is speaking lightly, almost joyfully, about prejudice and murder, concepts too heavy for a child of his age to grasp. It is because he doesn't understand the full impact of his words that Draco can speak so nonchalantly about such serious matters. Draco is not speaking his mind when he says these things; he is merely parroting what he's heard his parents say, looking to impress or frighten his peers. Lucius and Narcissa's twisted beliefs have been beaten into Draco's head since the day he was born. By now he can recite them back without even beginning to understand what he is saying.

Draco's biggest flaw, then, may not be that he is evil, but that he is a stubborn, ignorant child. He does not understand the true meaning behind his words. It is his romanticized view of the Dark Arts and his father's life that leads Draco into Voldemort's service, not a genuine understanding of what Voldemort stands for. Even Narcissa admits this when she seeks out Snape's help after Draco has been given the task of killing Dumbledore:

> [Bellatrix:] "The Dark Lord is granting him a great
> honor….[Draco] isn't shrinking away from his duty, he seems
> glad of a chance to prove himself, excited at the prospect—"
> Narcissa began to cry in earnest…"That's because he is
> sixteen and has no idea what lies in store!" [HBP, p. 33]

Narcissa is quite right. She raised her son to be a Death Eater without teaching him what service to the Dark Lord really meant. Draco had no idea what to expect when he entered Voldemort's service, and now he finds himself in over his head.

It is interesting to consider why Draco became a Death Eater. Yes, he was groomed for the role by his parents. But if he doesn't have what it takes to be a spy, Draco doesn't have what it takes to be a Death Eater either—and for much the same reasons.

Draco is a coward. Although Death Eaters hide behind their masks, theirs is truly a dangerous profession. Most Death Eaters end up in Azkaban or dead; being a Death Eater is not something to be entered into lightly. It is hard to picture Draco willingly facing the kinds of hazardous situations that Death Eaters must tackle. Being a Death Eater also means following orders, no matter how dangerous or distasteful those orders may be. Voldemort is not a wizard to be trifled with, and when he gives an order he expects it to be carried out flawlessly. Draco is used to giving orders, not following them. Draco either cannot or will not carry out his orders to kill Dumbledore; he is not willing to go to any lengths to make sure the Dark Lord is happy, even when his life and the lives of his family hang in the balance.

Besides being cowardly and unable to follow orders, Draco is boastful. Death Eaters need to work in secret, creating an atmosphere of terror with their horrible, seemingly random, acts. Draco likes to brag far too much for that. When the Chamber of Secrets is first opened and Mrs. Norris petrified, Draco anxiously pushed his way to the front of the crowd, yelling, "Enemies of the Heir, beware! You'll be next, Mudbloods!" [COS, p. 139]. Death Eaters need to be more subtle, not drawing attention to themselves at every opportunity. Even at the height of Voldemort's power, the Death Eaters did not work in the open. Draco, however, draws as much attention to himself as he possibly can. Even after becoming a Death Eater and being assigned to kill Dumbledore, he brags to his fellow Slytherins:

> "...I might not even be at Hogwarts next year....I might have—er—moved on to bigger and better things."
>
> ... "Do you mean—Him?"
>
> "...When the Dark Lord takes over, is he going to care how many O.W.L.s or N.E.W.T.s anyone's got?...It'll be all about the kind of service he received, the level of devotion he was shown." [HBP, p. 151]

In short, Draco is not Death Eater material. He has no idea what service to the Dark Lord actually entails. Initially he approaches it as though it were some sort of game—his regular bullying taken to a higher level. What he does not grasp immediately is that to be a Death Eater means to be willing to put it all on the line: to fight and die for Voldemort without a second thought. As Draco proves when he fails to kill Dumbledore, he is not willing to kill for Voldemort, and he certainly is not willing to die for him.

What Does Voldemort Really Want Him For?

We have explained why Draco wanted to join the Death Eaters, why he wanted to serve Voldemort at first. But why would Voldemort want Draco as a Death Eater? As Zabini points out in the passage quoted above, Draco is only sixteen years old and not fully qualified as a wizard. In addition, Draco is cowardly, unable to follow orders, boastful, and unwilling to go to any lengths to get the job done.

Draco also has a thirst for power, and he always looks out for number one. Dolores Umbridge notices this when she appoints Draco to the Inquisitorial Squad but refuses to trust him fully because she sees "the look of eagerness and greed" [OOTP, p. 749] that appears on his face at the prospect of gaining a bit of knowledge that may be used against her. If Umbridge is clever enough to understand that Draco always puts his own best interests first, surely Voldemort also knows that the boy cannot be trusted.

Why, then, does Voldemort accept Draco as a Death Eater, giving him the Dark Mark and assigning him to kill Dumbledore? Precisely because Voldemort knows that Draco will fail. Voldemort only wants Draco as leverage; he wants to use Draco as a tool to punish Lucius for failing to retrieve the prophecy from the Department of Mysteries:

> "That's why he's chosen Draco, isn't it?" [Narcissa] persisted.
> "To punish Lucius?"
>
> "If Draco succeeds," said Snape... "he will be honored above all others."
>
> "But he won't succeed!" sobbed Narcissa...
>
> [Snape says] "Lucius....failed to retrieve the prophecy into the bargain. Yes, the Dark Lord is angry..."
>
> "Then I am right, he has chosen Draco in revenge!" choked Narcissa. [HBP, pp. 33-34]

Draco is only given the task of killing Dumbledore in order to punish Lucius in the first place. Voldemort not only *expects* Draco to fail, he expects him to be killed in the process. As Narcissa says, "In other words, it doesn't matter to him if Draco is killed!" [HBP, p. 34].

What does all this mean? It means that Voldemort doesn't want Draco as a Death Eater any more than Draco wants to continue being a Death Eater. This is bad news for Draco, who is completely expendable in Voldemort's eyes. Draco was made a Death Eater because he could be used to incite fear in other, more valuable Death Eaters (Lucius and Narcissa). He is of no real value to the Dark Lord otherwise, and Voldemort will gladly dispose of him the moment he stops being of use.

What Will Happen to Draco If He Goes on the Run?

In the end, it is not Draco who kills Dumbledore, but Snape. Snape fulfills the vow he made to Narcissa, killing Dumbledore and saving Draco's life in the process. This will not sit well with Voldemort, who had hoped to see Draco killed, and who is just as cruel to his followers as he is to his enemies. Draco understands Voldemort's cruelty firsthand now and he will not be anxious to see that cruelty directed against himself. Snape may try to protect Draco as best he can, but with Dumbledore's death, Snape himself is a marked man and not in much of a position to guard Draco. Realizing that Voldemort no longer has any use for him, and that he is in danger as long as he remains with the Death Eaters, Draco will have no choice but to go on the run.

Motivated by the same fear that kept him in the ranks after his first two attempts to kill Dumbledore failed, Draco will go into hiding to avoid being killed outright in punishment or given another impossible task that will result in his death. Unfortunately for Draco, no one (with the possible exception of Snape) has ever defected from the Death Eaters and lived to tell the tale. Both Regulus Black and Igor Karkaroff left the Death Eaters, and both were tracked down and killed shortly thereafter. The Death Eaters quite literally have lifetime membership, death being the only tolerated means of departure. Draco's chances do not look good.

Will Draco Live to See the End of Book 7?

This is a topic of great debate. All evidence considered, Draco is in a very precarious situation. He is a young wizard, not yet fully qualified, and he is about to go on the run from one of the most powerful Dark Wizards the world has ever seen. Draco is terrified, and with good reason. Older, fully qualified witches and wizards have been murdered in Voldemort's quest for power. What chance does the spoiled, selfish son of a pair of Death Eaters have? As Remus Lupin says when discussing Karkaroff's murder: "Frankly, I'm surprised he stayed alive for even a year after deserting the Death Eaters; Sirius's brother, Regulus, only managed a few days as far as I can remember" [HBP, p. 106].

For the first time in his life, Draco is completely alone. His parents are no longer in a position to help him and he has no one else to turn to. Lucius is imprisoned in Azkaban. Narcissa has defied Voldemort's orders and entered into an Unbreakable Vow with Snape; she will be busy trying to save herself, once Voldemort finds out. Snape himself is a marked man who may not live to see the end of the war. Dumbledore is dead, and the kind of protection Draco needs at this point lies far beyond the bullying capabilities of Crabbe and Goyle. Draco once told Snape, "I've got older people on my side, better people" [HBP, p. 324]. It seems likely that he was referring to the Death Eaters he helped break into Hogwarts on the night that Dumbledore was murdered. But no Death Eater is going to side with Draco against Voldemort. The other Death Eaters will avoid or openly shun Draco rather than risk the Dark Lord's wrath. We have already explained why we do not believe that he will turn to the Order for protection. In short, Draco is without recourse.

The seventh book will show Draco standing alone against impossible odds. Throughout the series, Rowling, through Dumbledore, has emphasized the importance of choice: the value of choosing what is right over doing what is easy. While Draco was born into a family obsessed with the Dark Arts, he chose to follow in his parents' footsteps. He could have rebelled against his family's pureblood bigotry, as Sirius and Andromeda did. Instead, Draco blindly accepted what he was taught, never bothering to question or even fully comprehend the values his parents were teaching him. Draco took what he thought would be the easy path to power and privilege. He chose to become a Death Eater, and, chances are, he will pay for that choice with his life.

What is Draco's destiny? He will not rebel against Voldemort and the Death Eaters; he will run from them in fear. He entered into Voldemort's service without completely understanding the risks, and he will pay for his negligence with his life. It would take nothing less than a miracle for Draco to survive his time as a Death Eater. Draco will not be safe until Voldemort and every one of his followers is gone. Even if Draco lives long enough to witness Voldemort's demise, he will pay for his betrayal. One of the more fanatical Death Eaters—Bellatrix, perhaps—will see to that. One way or another, Draco's time is very nearly up.

Can any good come of Draco's death? Yes: Draco's death may render Lucius and Narcissa useless to Voldemort. Draco is their only son. Narcissa loves Draco a great deal, and Lucius obviously wished to groom Draco to follow in his footsteps. Their son's murder would devastate them both. That he was murdered by Voldemort or one of the Death Eaters would only add to their shock and sorrow. If Lucius and Narcissa even stayed with the Death Eaters after Draco's death, it would be in a much diminished capacity as their loyalty would be broken. If that happens, Draco's death may have a higher purpose after all. Not only will it remove Draco himself from the fight, but it will take out two of Voldemort's most faithful followers. That may just give the Order the advantage it needs to destroy the Death Eaters once and for all.

Love

Relationships gave us by far the biggest talking points—and, let's be honest, the biggest arguments as well—of the first five books. Yes, people like to swap theories about whether Snape is good or evil, and whether Malfoy will turn out OK in the end, but if you really want to get people going, you mention love. Would it be Harry/Hermione? Or Ron/Hermione? The fights have been legendary…

Then J.K.R. did something that nobody could have anticipated. She told us the answer, as these quotes reveal:

> **ES:** *We thought it was clearer than ever that Harry and Ginny are an item and Ron and Hermione—although we think you made it painfully obvious in the first five books.*
>
> **J.K.R.:** *So do I!* [MuggleNet/TLC interview, 2005]
>
> **J.K.R.:** *I will say, that yes, I personally feel—well it's going to be clear once people have read Book 6. I mean, that's it. It's done, isn't it? We know. Yes, we do now know that it's Ron and Hermione.* [MuggleNet/TLC interview, 2005]

The Ron/Hermione pairing was no surprise; the previous five books were littered with very strong clues and romantic tension. The Harry/Ginny pairing was equally expected, although quite a few readers saw Harry being pushed in the direction of Luna Lovegood towards the end of OOTP. The surprising thing is that J.K.R. decided to tell us all a book early, and settle the argument once and for all.

Before HBP, this would have been a chapter about who was going to end up with whom. Too late now. Now that we know who likes each other, the question is, Will it all work out for them?

The Ones That Didn't Work Out

Harry, Ginny, Ron, and Hermione have all arrived where they are via some previous—and in many cases, unwise—relationships. All of these have one thing in common: They belong in the past, and they're not coming back. It's useful to reflect on these past experiences for a number of reasons. In many cases they have provided valuable practice in dealing with the opposite sex, and in others it's simply a good thing to show that there's no chance whatsoever of anything from the past being re-ignited.

Harry

Harry's ex is Cho Chang, who he has a crush on for two years before finally getting together with in OOTP. He really likes her at the time, and can't even look at her without getting all weird.

> *Harry saw Cho laughing and felt the familiar swooping sensation in his stomach, as though he had missed a step going downstairs.* [OOTP, p. 454]

He tries to ask her out to the Yule Ball in GOF, but Cedric Diggory gets there first [GOF, p. 397]. He finally manages to get together with her a year later [OOTP, pp. 456-57]. It all goes horribly wrong, however: a disastrous date in Hogsmeade [OOTP, pp. 561-62] is fol-

lowed by an argument about Cho's friend Marietta betraying the
D.A. [OOTP, p. 637], and that's the end. By the time he catches the
Hogwarts Express back home at the end of the year, he has lost all
interest in her.

> *Wanting to impress Cho seemed to belong to a past that was*
> *no longer quite connected with him.* [OOTP, p. 865]

Harry's interest in Cho is definitely over, and it's doubtful
whether he learned a great deal along the way, except for possibly a
few pointers about what not to do.

Ron

Ron goes out with Lavender Brown for a few months in HBP,
although it's pretty clear that he does so simply because the opportunity was there, rather than because of any great enthusiasm. Even
at the start of their relationship he is far more interested in the fact
that Hermione has asked Cormac McLaggen to Horace Slughorn's
Christmas party than he is in kissing his girlfriend [HBP, p. 315]. By
the start of spring he has taken to trying to avoid her [HBP, p. 469],
and they inevitably split up shortly afterwards.

The experience with Lavender no doubt helps Ron to improve
his kissing technique (which was very shaky to start with [HBP, p.
287]), but the main purpose of this relationship is to show him how
shallow it is and how much more fulfillment he could find elsewhere. As J.K.R. said:

> *He's had the meaningless physical experience—let's face it,*
> *his emotions were never deeply engaged with Lavender—and*
> *he's realized that that is ultimately not what he wants, which*
> *takes him a huge emotional step forward.* [MuggleNet/TLC
> interview, 2005]

For Ron, the Lavender experience is a sharp and very necessary
learning curve.

Hermione

Hermione attracts the attention of Viktor Krum during GOF. Unsurprisingly she is flattered by the attentions of an 18-year-old international Quidditch player and accompanies him to the Yule Ball [GOF, p. 422]. At some point, according to Ginny Weasley, she goes as far as to kiss him [HBP, p. 288], and Viktor reveals that he has never felt about anyone else the way he feels about her [GOF, p. 512]. Hermione, though she likes him, does not feel the same way (to her credit, she does her best to let him down gently). She politely declines his invitation to visit him in Bulgaria over the summer, and by the end of the year is showing a distinct lack of enthusiasm. This is her response when he asks her to go with him so he can say goodbye:

> *"Oh.... yes...alright," said Hermione.* [GOF, p.725]

She nevertheless continues to correspond with him, becoming a penpal rather than a girlfriend [OOTP, p. 460], and that is now as far as their relationship goes. The main thing that it achieves, just like Ron's experience with Lavender, is to show Hermione that her true affections lie elsewhere.

Ginny

Ginny goes out with a Ravenclaw named Michael Corner during her fourth year, and then Dean Thomas in her fifth year. In both cases she ends up with them only because she has begun to give up hope that things will work out with Harry. As she later explains to Harry:

> *"...Hermione told me to get on with life, maybe go out with some other people, relax a bit around you, because I never used to be able to talk if you were in the room, remember?"* [HBP, p. 647]

These relationships certainly help her to relax in Harry's company, and therefore play a major part in the two of them getting together. Now she's been out with Harry, however, both of her flings lie firmly in the past.

The past is one thing, but the future is another. Whatever happened in the past, we know who likes each other now. The big question is, will it all work out?

Harry and Hermione: The One That Never Was

Now that J.K.R. has confirmed the Harry/Ginny and Ron/Hermione pairings, it is unnecessary to go into great detail about the relationship that never was. However, in the context of readers' reactions to potential romance, nothing stirred up the emotions of many quite like the Harry/Hermione ship. This in itself is more of a mystery, as a few simple questions reveal all we need to know about why this particular pairing was always a non-starter.

If Hermione loved Harry, why was she so eager to get him together with Cho and then Ginny?

When Harry managed to finally kiss Cho, Hermione was delighted, and also very anxious that he should seize the initiative and ask her out properly.

> *"What if he doesn't want to ask her?" said Ron, who had been watching Harry with an unusually shrewd expression on his face.*
>
> *"Don't be silly," said Hermione vaguely. "Harry's liked her for ages, haven't you, Harry?"* [OOTP, p. 460]

Her reaction to Harry kissing Ginny for the first time was even more obvious.

> *Harry looked over the top of Ginny's head to see Dean Thomas holding a shattered glass in his hand, and Romilda Vane looking as though she might throw something. Hermione was beaming, but Harry's eyes sought Ron.* [HBP, p. 534]

Hermione had no interest in going out with Harry herself, and was purely and simply interested in Harry being happy.

Why was it Ron and not Harry who had a problem with Hermione attending the Yule Ball with Krum?

Both Ron and Harry made a similar mess of finding a partner for the Yule Ball, both failing to get the partner they wanted. It wasn't Harry who wanted to go with Hermione, though—it was Ron, and he was outraged that she had already agreed to go with someone else [GOF, p. 421]. As Harry said during the Ball:

> *"Ron," said Harry quietly, "I haven't got a problem with Hermione coming with Krum—"*
> *But Ron ignored Harry too.* [GOF, p. 423]

These are not the words of someone who secretly wanted to be with Hermione. As for Hermione herself, she was just disappointed that Ron hadn't asked her before Krum did, and she wasted no time in advising him to ask her properly next time there was a Ball [GOF, p. 432]. Again, tellingly, she told Harry no such thing.

But why do Harry and Hermione get along so well? They always seem to be pairing up as friends but never fight or anything.

That's just the point. At the age Harry, Ron, and Hermione are at, getting along so well is the sign of a lack of sexual tension, not a sign that they'd secretly like to be kissing each other. Ron and Hermione fall out all the time because they care so much about what the other one thinks, and they take the slightest hint of a rejection straight to heart. Harry and Hermione are not on that knife edge: they are simply friends, and friends don't fall out like that. The last word on this should be left to J.K.R.

> *Do Harry and Hermione have a date?*
>
> ***J.K.R.:*** *No! They're very platonic friends. But I won't answer for anyone else—nudge, nudge, wink, wink.* [NPR Radio, 1999]

J.K.R. is the author, and she told us straight. After that, it has always been clear that Harry/Hermione was not a realistic possibility.

And so we know about the past, we know what was never going to happen, and we know who does end up together. But will it all work out?

Harry and Ginny

It's not a secret that Ginny has always liked Harry. She has a crush on him from the moment she meets him, the first time Harry visits The Burrow:

> *At that moment there was a diversion in the form of a small, red-headed figure in a long nightdress, who appeared in the kitchen, gave a small squeal, and ran out again.*
>
> *"Ginny," said Ron in an undertone to Harry. "My sister. She's been talking about you all summer."* [COS, p. 35]

At the time, Harry is twelve and Ginny is almost eleven. And from that point on, she turns scarlet and runs away whenever she encounters Harry. But at the beginning of Book 5, she suddenly changes. Her first meeting with him in OOTP goes like this:

> *"Oh hello, Harry!" said Ron's younger sister, Ginny, brightly.*
> *"I thought I heard your voice."* [OOTP, p. 69]

The reason for the change is simple: She has pretty much given up. Harry is still looking all misty-eyed at Cho and hasn't given Ginny a thought for the past three years. Ginny, for her part, has discussed the situation with Hermione and has decided that it's really time for her to move on [HBP, p. 647].

At the time, Ginny's decision to look elsewhere looks like an admission of defeat. In fact, it turns out to have the opposite effect. Ginny has always been a spirited, likeable girl, but she hasn't been able to be herself around Harry. Suddenly free of the crippling embarrassment she has always felt when she is around him, she starts going out with Michael Corner and Harry and Ginny became real friends for the first time. They hang out together in Grimmauld Place; she joins the D.A. (bringing her boyfriend with her); and she even fights in the battle at the Department of Mysteries [OOTP, ch. 35].

Harry never looks at her in a romantic way, of course; he is still fixated on Cho. But their friendship lays the foundation for what is to come. Ron, for one, does his best to push the two together when Ginny splits up with Michael and Harry's crush on Cho has petered out:

> *"Just choose someone—better—next time."*
> *He cast Harry an oddly furtive look as he said it.* [OOTP, p. 866]

But Ginny has given up on Harry, and she chooses Dean Thomas instead. Ron is none too pleased.

In terms of friendship, Harry and Ginny are closer than ever at the end of Book 5. In terms of romance, they are farther apart than ever. The one thing that's needed to bring them together is a bit of encouragement from Harry. Ginny could be easily persuaded back, if only she could see a sign that Harry liked her…

When Did He Start to Like Her?

It's impossible to say exactly when Harry first notices Ginny in a romantic way, but it's not hard to guess. By the end of OOTP, Harry has lost all interest in Cho Chang. He spends most of the summer at The Burrow, where he hangs out with Ginny and her brothers all day long. Ginny has developed into a confident, attractive fifteen-year-old, and although J.K.R. doesn't drop any new hints, this is undoubtedly when something changes inside Harry's mind.

We see the first tiny piece of evidence of this change on the Hogwarts Express, when Harry suggests that he and Ginny share a compartment. Ginny has agreed to meet Dean on the train and turns him down:

> *He felt a strange twinge of annoyance as she walked away,*
> *her long red hair dancing behind her.* [HBP, p. 136]

It's small, but it's the first clue that Harry's heart has changed. The clue is confirmed not long afterwards, during Harry's first potions lesson of the year. Professor Slughorn has brewed up a cauldron of Amortentia, the most powerful love potion in the world, which smells to each person of whatever it is they find attractive. What Harry smells is:

> ... *treacle tart, the woody smell of a broomstick handle, and something flowery he thought he might have smelled at the Burrow.* [HBP, p. 183]

J.K.R. doesn't wait long to reveal what that smell is:

> *"Hang on," said a voice close to Harry's left ear and he caught a sudden waft of that flowery smell.... He looked around and saw that Ginny had joined them.* [HBP, p. 192]

Harry hasn't yet realized what's going on, though he does get annoyed during the next trip to Hogsmeade when he thinks of Ginny and Dean getting cozy in Madam Puddifoot's café. But he's forced to confront the issue head-on when he and Ron run slap-bang into Dean and Ginny kissing:

> *It was as though something large and scaly erupted into life in Harry's stomach, clawing at his insides: Hot blood seemed to flood his brain, so that all thought was extinguished, replaced by a savage urge to jinx Dean into a jelly.* [HBP, p. 286]

Harry does his very best to convince himself that the jealousy which engulfs him at this point is nothing more than a protective feeling towards a friend who is more like a sister, but in his heart he knows he has already lost the battle. When Harry likes somebody, he really likes them, and his affection for Ginny is suddenly about as deep as you can get [HBP, p. 286].

So Ginny has got what she's wanted for so long. But now that she's going out with Dean Thomas, perhaps she won't be interested after all.

What Does Ginny Think?

Ginny seems quite happy with Dean and with life in general throughout the whole of the first term in HBP. Giving up on Harry no doubt hurt a bit in the short term, but she does really seem to be into Dean. Up until Christmas, at least, she has no idea about Harry's change of heart.

Harry spends the holidays with the Weasleys, and maybe Ginny picks up on something then, because when they get back to school, Harry can't help noticing that she doesn't seem all that enthusiastic about seeing Dean [HBP, p. 352]. That may just be wishful thinking on Harry's part, but one way or another, Ginny and Dean aren't getting along as well as they used to. Shortly afterwards, Harry is rather overzealous in his attempts to find out why they quarrelled after Cormac McLaggen knocked Harry out during a game of Quidditch [HBP, p. 423]. Hermione is quick to notice Harry's interest, and her reaction reveals two things: She didn't know about his change of heart before, but she knows now.

Everyone knows that Hermione and Ginny are great friends, so it's probably no coincidence that from this point on, Ginny's relationship with Dean goes into a sharp decline. It's probably true to say that at the height of her relationship with Dean, Ginny was very happy; she might not have split up with Dean even if she had known that Harry was interested in her. But now, with the relationship going downhill anyway, the new situation with Harry is the little shove that is needed to push it over the edge. They split up just a couple of weeks later, and Ginny (unlike Dean) is apparently rather happy about it [HBP, p. 514].

It took the best part of five years, but Harry and Ginny are finally in the same place: They both want to go out with each other at the same time. But Harry doesn't manage to ask Ginny out very quickly; he spends most of the time before he gets around to kissing her worrying that someone else might ask her instead [HBP, p. 519]. He needn't worry, though. Yes, there is every chance that someone might ask Ginny out, but there is no chance whatsoever that she will say yes to anyone but Harry.

Ginny explained to Harry after Dumbledore's funeral that she had never really given up on him, and she was telling the truth. OK, it wasn't going so well with Dean anyway, but as soon as she knew that Harry was interested at last, her mind was made up. This is shown by the fact that when they do finally get together, nobody asks anybody else [HBP, p. 533]. They both just know it is right.

Does Harry Really Split Up with Ginny?

Harry and Ginny are happy, of course, but their happiness doesn't last long. Dumbledore's death, together with the knowledge that he must destroy Voldemort's Horcruxes, make Harry realize that he can't continue to go out with Ginny. If he did, he would be putting her life in danger, as Voldemort has a history of using the loved ones of his enemies as bait. So at Dumbledore's funeral he calls it all off—or at least, he tries to [HBP, p. 647]. There is a distinct lack of finality about the way it happens, however. Ginny ends up telling him why she likes him so much, and Harry walks out because he can't bear to listen.

He has forgotten one important thing, however. He is going to be spending at least some time in Ginny's company before he sets out on his Horcrux quest—they will both be at Bill and Fleur's wedding. Ron and Hermione remind him of this in the last few paragraphs of HBP. Harry really likes Ginny, and Ginny really likes Harry. It'll be hard enough for both of them even if they aren't seeing each other. For them both to be at The Burrow will be too much.

Yes, they've split up for the moment, and they won't officially get back together at the wedding because the reason Harry called it off is still valid. What the wedding will do, however, is remind them both how much they like each other. They will move on with the understanding that if Harry returns victorious from his quest (which he will), Ginny will be there waiting for him. And this time there will be nothing to stop them from staying together.

So did Harry really split up with Ginny? Sort of. He did, but it isn't going to last.

The Future for Harry and Ginny

The good news is that the future looks pretty bright. Harry will defeat Voldemort, Ginny will wait for him, and the two of them will end up together. End of story.

Harry and Ginny are uniquely well matched, having been through four separate stages of their relationship: Ginny loves Harry; Harry loves Ginny; genuine friendship with no desire on either side; and finally being together. The fact that each one has independently fallen for the other, and that they have managed to fit in a spot of close friendship as well, makes them easily the strongest fledgling couple in the entire series.

After all he's been through, Harry deserves a bit of luck and someone great to come back to, and that's exactly what he will get. All fairytales end this way, and Ginny will be Harry's "happily ever after."

Ron and Hermione

It's hard to imagine a pairing more different from Harry and Ginny, who very publicly liked the pants off each other (albeit at different times), and who, as far as we know, have barely exchanged an angry word even during Harry's "unreasonable" phase in OOTP. Ron and Hermione, on the other hand, are constantly bickering at each other. They would never admit that they like each other, and yet each one becomes insanely jealous the moment they see the other one as much as glancing at someone else.

There's no doubt, it's been a long and rocky road for Ron and Hermione, and they still haven't done a Harry and Ginny and gotten together properly. We know they like each other, of course, but in the world of Ron Weasley, matters with girls are always more complicated than they need to be, even if he is less immature these days.

So will they get together and stay together? To answer that, let's look at the background to their relationship.

He Notices Her (Finally)

GOF is the big book for Ron and Hermione, littered as it is with what J.K.R. has called "anvil-sized hints" about their feelings for each other [MuggleNet/TLC interview, 2005]. There is nothing before POA, at least in the books. The COS movie has Hermione hugging Harry at the end but only shaking hands with Ron because she feels awkward with him, but this scene was invented for the movie; it doesn't appear anywhere else. In the book, Ron is far too immature to take an interest in girls at this stage, and Hermione is nursing a major crush on Gilderoy Lockhart anyway [COS, p. 228].

POA sees Ron and Hermione constantly quarrelling, which is the first subtle hint of some sort of bond. To get the action really flowing, however, it takes the introduction (in GOF) of someone who catches Ron's eye for the first time in his life. That someone is Fleur Delacour. Up until this point, Hermione has been willing to put up with Ron not noticing her, as long as he doesn't notice anyone else. He most certainly does notice Fleur, however:

> *"I'm telling you, that's not a normal girl!" said Ron, leaning sideways so he could keep a clear view of her. "They don't make them like that at Hogwarts!"* [GOF, pp. 252-53]

That puts Hermione's nose out of joint, but it also makes up her mind for her. It makes her realize that it's Ron she wants, and that she'd better do something about it. Her feelings are very clear when Ron is fortunate enough to get a kiss from Fleur following the second task of the Triwizard Tournament.

> *Fleur swooped down on him too and kissed him. Hermione looked simply furious.* [GOF, p. 506]

Unfortunately for her, however, Ron is still too immature to notice her at first, and when he does notice her, he is too immature to admit it, even to himself.

The Yule Ball

At the Yule Ball, the matter comes to a head. Hermione, no doubt, harbors some sort of hope that Ron will ask her to the ball. Needless to say, he doesn't. Instead, he announces loudly in front of her that he hopes he and Harry won't end up with a "pair of trolls" [GOF, p. 394]. When Viktor Krum asks Hermione himself, she accepts, and is quick to let Ron know what she thinks of his failure to ask her.

> *"Just because it's taken you three years to notice, Ron, doesn't mean no one else has spotted I'm a girl!"* [GOF, p. 400]

At first Ron doesn't believe it. But he has to believe it when she arrives with Krum at the ball, and this is the moment when he first realizes that he feels something for her in return. He spends the entire ball staring at Hermione, and then being rude to her, Krum, his date, and just about everyone else. Then he has a blazing spat with her in the Gryffindor common room [GOF, p. 400]. At this point, Hermione tells him exactly how she feels in a way that even Ron would have to struggle to misunderstand:

> *"Next time there's a ball, ask me before someone else does, and not as a last resort!"* [GOF, p. 432]

Ron does figure out the score after this, but he doesn't let on, as in truth he feels out of his league with the whole situation. If he didn't want Harry to find out, however, he should have hidden the figurine of Viktor Krum that he smashed up more carefully [GOF, p. 444].

The stage is now set for the next phase of the Ron/Hermione relationship, a stage that lasts for around two and a half years. We refer to the bickering, jealous phase.

Bickering

In many ways, it's almost as if Ron and Hermione are going out already: They're close, they argue, they bicker, they make up. It's only the kissing that's missing. Although this is likely to be a million miles from what Hermione was really looking for, she puts up with it anyway—and for an awfully long time—because she knows that in terms of maturity, Ron is a long way behind her. What's more, her actions throughout OOTP, where she shows no interest at all in any other Hogwarts boys, suggest that she is willing to wait until he grows up. Further evidence of this can be found in HBP, where she tries to get Ron back rather than looking for someone else when he starts going out with Lavender Brown [HBP, p. 317].

Their bickering is usually about members of the opposite sex. If Ron looks at Fleur (or goes out with Lavender), or if Hermione seems close to Viktor, trouble is in the air. Viktor really likes Hermione, of course, so much so that he invites her to visit him in Bulgaria [GOF, p. 513] and confronts Harry about his own friendship with her [GOF, p. 552]. But Hermione is sharp enough to have figured out Ron's true intentions, no matter how hard he tries to hide them. He's the one she really wants, so Krum is out, no matter how good he is at Quidditch.

Ron doesn't think he is giving much away, but he gets so bent out of shape every time Hermione so much as mentions Viktor that even Harry notices what's going on [OOTP, p. 461]. It takes Ron a long time to grow up, however, and it's to Hermione's credit that she is prepared to tough it out. The whole of OOTP goes by in this fashion, with just a few barbed comments from Hermione when Ron has been particularly annoying:

> *"Just because you've got the emotional range of a teaspoon doesn't mean we all have," said Hermione nastily.* [OOTP, p. 459]

They go on bickering through the whole of HBP. Ron starts to go out with Lavender because he knows she'll say yes, even though he doesn't enjoy it very much. Hermione carries on doing her best to get things moving by asking Ron to go to Professor Slughorn's Christmas party with her, but it's at this point that Ron and Lavender get together, and so she ends up asking Cormac McLaggen instead, just to annoy him [HBP, p. 317]. This it does, so much so that it takes Ron nearly being killed by poisoned mead to make them friends again [HBP, p. 423]. In other words, it's business as usual.

The Lavender interlude is important, though. It's a meaningless, purely physical relationship, and it teaches Ron that this isn't what he wants. At last he has matured enough to admit what he does want, and Hermione's wait is nearly over.

The Future for Ron and Hermione

The final Ron/Hermione action in HBP is more subtle than what happens when Harry and Ginny get together. Ron holds Hermione as she cries at Dumbledore's funeral, while not far away Harry does his best to split up with Ginny. It's hardly conclusive, and people would still be arguing about it if J.K.R. hadn't already told us that the Ron/Hermione pairing was a goer.

Their relationship is very different from Harry and Ginny's, of course. They fight, they bicker, and they seem to be ignoring each other as often as not. But at the end of the day they love each other, and (despite the odd distraction) they have waited a long time for each other. In the end, it will prove to be time well spent.

Ron and Hermione's relationship will be a huge roller coaster compared to a lot of others, and there'll be a lot of tears and shouting on both sides. In fact, it will be just like it's always been, but with a bit of kissing thrown in for good measure. Overall it will make them happy, and just like Harry/Ginny, this one will last. They've waited so long for one another that now that they're finally together, they won't throw it away.

The Others

The Harry/Ginny and Ron/Hermione pairings are the big two, but there are some other relationships that are also interesting to look at. Unfortunately, most of them involve people who are very much at risk of dying in Book 7, and it's almost certain that not all of those people will make it out alive. You can't live happily ever after if you're dead. However, some might make it all the way, and so here we take a brief look at the future of the other relationships that have been hinted at.

Remus and Tonks

Of all the relationships outside the Harry/Ginny and Ron/Hermione pairings, Remus and Tonks have the best chance of making it through—if they both survive. Unfortunately, for reasons discussed elsewhere, there's every chance that at least one of them will fail to make it. They're a well-matched couple, with both being committed members of the Order of the Phoenix, and both dedicated to the fight against Voldemort. It is just this devotion to the cause that is likely to bring Remus' life to an early end, however.

Tonks is clearly very smitten with him, so much so that she falls into a deep depression when Remus initially says that they can't be together.

> *Harry thought she looked drawn, even ill, and there was*
> *something forced in her smile. Certainly her appearance*
> *was less colorful than usual without her customary shade*
> *of bubble-gum-pink hair.* [HBP, p. 82]

Remus' intentions in turning her down are honorable: He likes her just as much as she likes him, but is determined that she shouldn't end up with a werewolf for a boyfriend.

> *"And I've told you a million times," said [Remus] Lupin,*
> *refusing to meet her eyes, staring at the floor, "that I am too*
> *old for you, too poor... too dangerous...."* [HBP, p. 624]

Remus is finally convinced to relent by Fleur's determination to still marry Bill Weasley despite him being savaged by Fenrir Greyback [HBP, p. 623]. At Dumbledore's funeral, they are clearly an item.

> *"...Tonks, her hair miraculously returned to vividest pink;*
> *Remus Lupin, with whom she seemed to be holding hands..."*
> [HBP, p. 641]

They are finally together, and they are happy. But sadly their happiness could be short-lived. After all, both Remus and Tonks are on the front line of the battle against the Death Eaters. The odds would already be against them if just one or the other were heavily involved in the fight, but with both of them getting shot at by Voldemort's army, the future looks awfully bleak for this couple.

Hagrid and Olympe

The Hagrid and Olympe pairing is another that contains a character—Hagrid—who is unlikely to make it to the end of Book 7, which necessarily casts a cloud over this potential relationship. Even if Hagrid does defy the odds and make it through, it looks none too hopeful anyway.

Hagrid likes Olympe the moment he sees her, and quickly takes to dressing up in his best clothes and trying to tame his hair with axle grease when she's around [GOF, p. 263]. Initially, Olympe is interested only in finding out more information about the Triwizard Tournament, but she slowly begins to warm to him, and by the time of the Yule Ball they are getting along well [GOF, p. 418]. Hagrid comes close to blowing it entirely towards the end of that evening by (accurately, it should be said) calling her a half-giant, and it isn't until later in the spring that they're back on friendly terms [GOF, p. 718]. Olympe seems genuinely upset in the interim, however, suggesting that she is beginning to share Hagrid's feelings [OOTP, ch. 31].

The two go on a mission to the giants in the summer, apparently now the best of friends, and Hagrid speaks about her in glowing terms upon his return.

> "...I'll tell yeh this, she's not afraid of roughin' it, Olympe. Yeh know, she's a fine, well-dressed woman, an' knowin' where we was goin' I wondered 'ow she'd feel abou' clamberin' over boulders an' sleepin' in caves an' tha', bu' she never complained once." [OOTP, p. 424]

This, however, is the last we hear of her. She's the Headmistress of Beauxbatons, and so her chances to see Hagrid are very few and far between, but even so it does seem to be a sudden and very complete shutdown in relations. Even when she attends Dumbledore's funeral, there's no mention of any interaction between the two [HBP, p. 641].

Therefore, even in the unlikely event of Hagrid surviving Book 7, his relationship with Olympe seems to be in the past.

Draco and Pansy

Draco and Pansy go back just as far as Ron and Hermione. Pansy's affection for Draco is first seen following Hagrid's inaugural lesson as Care of Magic Creatures teacher. Draco insults Buckbeak the Hippogriff and gets gored for his trouble, and Pansy is in tears [POA, p. 118]. Malfoy clearly likes her as well, enough to ask her to the Yule Ball the following year, anyway [GOF, p. 414]. By the start of their sixth year, Draco lies with his head in Pansy's lap on the Hogwarts Express, and Pansy looks at him in admiration [HBP, p. 149].

This seems to suggest that the two of them have been an item for some time, but you can bet against it lasting. Draco has gone over his head in the Death Eaters, and has failed his task to kill Dumbledore [HBP, p. 595]. As described in Chapter 6, we believe he is about to go on the run, before being tracked down and brutally killed. It seems that Pansy is never going to see her boyfriend again.

Neville and Luna

This is the dark horse of the lot, for many reasons. The most prominent of these is that J.K.R. appears to have written off the relationship on her website:

> *The Luna/Neville shippers are much less vehement and scary than the Harry/Hermione, Ron/Hermione tribes, so I hope I won't receive too much hate mail for quashing this rumour. I see Neville and Luna as very different kinds of people and*

*while they share a certain isolation within Hogwarts, I don't
think that's enough to foster true love.* [J.K.R. website]

That would be it for the Neville/Luna ship, except for the fact
that she was answering a question about whether they would hook
up specifically in HBP. She made no comment as to what might
happen after that.

Admittedly, the answer does contain an assertion that the two
are rather incompatible. Even so, HBP sees them being pushed
towards each other as the last remaining loyal members of the D.A.,
even if there haven't been any firm hints of romance. The last
action of the book sees them together once more as Luna helps
Neville at Dumbledore's funeral, following Neville getting injured
in the recent battle with the Death Eaters.

*...With a great rush of affection for both of them, Harry saw
Neville being helped into a seat by Luna. Neville and Luna
alone of the D.A. had responded to Hermione's summons the
night that Dumbledore had died, and Harry knew why: They
were the ones who had missed the D.A. most.* [HBP, pp. 641-42]

While this is hardly concrete evidence that the two are going to
end up together, it still qualifies as heavy hinting. The other good
news for both is that they have a low risk of getting the axe. Neville
will get his revenge on Bellatrix Lestrange, and Luna won't be in
the thick of the action. It's not a certainty, but this one might just
make it all the way.

Life Debts and Where They Will Lead Wormtail

The concept of a wizarding life debt is introduced at the end of POA, and although it is barely mentioned again, it will become absolutely vital in Book 7. It is really true to say that the entire outcome of the Harry/Voldemort war hinges on a wizarding debt (or two).

It's probably best left to Dumbledore, wise as he was, to describe what a life debt is all about:

> *"When one wizard saves another wizard's life, it creates a certain bond between them....This is magic at its deepest, its most impenetrable....the time may come when you will be very glad you saved Pettigrew's life."* [POA, p. 427]

And that's it. A simple definition and then goodbye. Nobody mentions life debts again for the next three books, although in that time many debts have been created. Some of them won't make the slightest bit of difference to the story, but the implications of those that do are enormous.

A Debt between Friends

A life debt is contracted when one wizard saves the life of another, and the magic of the bond ensures that the debt must be repaid. Since Hogwarts and the wizarding world are pretty dangerous places to be, friends end up saving each other's lives all the time. And thus many life debts are created:

Ron is indebted to Harry:
For saving Ron's life when he had drunk poisoned mead in Horace Slughorn's office [HBP, p. 398].

Hermione is indebted to Harry:
For interrupting a Death Eater's Killing Curse in the battle at the Department of Mysteries [OOTP, p. 789].

Dumbledore is indebted to Snape:
For saving his life when he had been critically injured by the ring Horcrux [HBP, p. 503].

The bottom line, however, is that none of these debts is really important. Friends will save a friend's life when it comes down to it anyway, and they don't need a life debt to make them do it. At the end of the day, a debt between enemies is much more fun.

A Debt between Enemies

A debt between enemies is the sort of debt that really makes a difference, the sort of debt that makes people change the way they behave. More life debts have been created between enemies than you might think, and two of them are absolutely vital to the plot of Book 7. The full list looks like this:

Snape is indebted to James Potter:

For preventing Snape from being attacked by Remus Lupin in werewolf form after Sirius had tricked him into going to find him [POA, p. 357].

Harry is indebted to Snape:

For saving Harry from being thrown to his death from his broom during his first game of Quidditch for Gryffindor [SS, pp. 190 & 289].

Crouch Jr. is indebted to Crouch Sr.:

For springing Crouch Jr. out of Azkaban, where he was dying [GOF, p. 684].

Pettigrew is indebted to Harry:

For stopping Sirius and Remus from killing him in the Shrieking Shack, in revenge for his betrayal of the Potters [POA, p. 375].

The first of these life debts, between Snape and James Potter, is an interesting one. Snape told Voldemort about Trelawney's prophecy, which led to Voldemort killing James and Lily. This would seem to contradict the life-debt magic since Snape was indirectly responsible for this murder. But Snape did not know to whom the prophecy referred. When he finally realized that it targeted the Potters, he tried to save them by defecting from the Death Eaters and telling Dumbledore all he knew. But it was too late. James and Lily were killed, and he had failed to fulfill his debt. But the important thing is that he *did* try to save them.

The debt that Harry owes to Snape is a vital one. Its effects could have Harry trying to save Snape in Book 7 (see the Snape chapter for more information on this debt). The third debt, the one between Crouch Jr. and Crouch Sr., gives us a surprising insight into the nature of life debts. But the fourth debt, between Pettigrew and Harry, is the big one. It's the debt that Dumbledore was talking about when he explained how the magic works, and the one that has been brushed under the carpet since the end of POA, in the hope that we'll forget all about it. Not a chance! Wormtail's debt to Harry is big business, and Dumbledore, who was rarely wrong, hit the nail bang on the head during his explanation: "The time may come when you will be very glad you saved Pettigrew's life" [POA, p. 427].

The debt in question hasn't greatly changed Peter's behavior yet, although you can see its subtle effects whenever he encounters Harry: He doesn't even dare to look him in the face [GOF, p. 639]. But the time is coming, and when it comes, the effect it will have on the final outcome of Harry's war with Voldemort will be huge. We even have a promise from J.K.R. on this one:

> *Will Wormtail ever pay Harry back?*
>
> *J.K.R.: You'll see... Keep reading!* [World Book Day, 2004]

And whenever J.K.R. starts to get evasive like this, you can bet your life that somebody's hitting on a nerve.

Binding?

But before we get into the Wormtail situation, let's take a quick look at the third debt—the one between the two Crouches, father and son. Why? Because it teaches us something very important about the nature of the magic in question.

The thing about Crouch Jr. is that he killed his father [GOF, p. 690]. And he did it after his father had saved his life. He *should* have been bound by a life debt, and so have been quite unable to kill the person he was indebted to. But he wasn't. He murdered his father without a second thought. So how did he do it?

He managed it because a life debt is not created when a wizard saves the life of another. It is created when a wizard *feels indebted to* another for saving his or her life. The magic is set by the feeling of owing one's life to someone, not by the physical act of saving that took place. There is a subtle difference, but it's very important. If you don't feel indebted to the person who saved you, if you genuinely don't care about what they did, if you feel no emotion about it, then no debt is created.

Barty Crouch Jr. is a special kind of slimeball. He truly loves the acts of torture and murder that he commits in Voldemort's name. He has no remorse, no regret, no feelings for those he kills and maims. And he has no feelings for the man who saved his life, even though that man was his own father. In the very special case of Barty Crouch Jr. there is no life debt, because he is so cold he is unable to feel anything.

So a life debt is binding, but if you are detached enough to feel nothing, the debt is not created in the first place. On the other side of the fence is Peter Pettigrew. When Harry stepped in to save him, he flung his arms around Harry's knees, muttering "thank you" over and over again.

If he'd been a little more like Barty, he might have avoided creating a debt. But Peter Pettigrew clings to life like a limpet, and the chances are zero that he felt nothing when Harry saved his life. And so he contracted a life debt to Harry, and in the war that's brewing, it will lead not only to his own destruction, but to a whole lot more trouble for his Dark master to boot.

The Wormtail Debt

The way Peter picked up his life debt is pretty well-known, but it's worth quickly going over the major points. Wormtail was, of course, the spy who passed secrets from the Order of the Phoenix to Lord Voldemort, something that he did for over a year [POA, p. 374]. The information he passed on after he was made Secret Keeper for the Potters when they went into hiding led to their murder, for which he successfully managed to frame Sirius Black before faking his own death.

Peter then went into hiding for 12 years, using his animagus form to pose as a rat. Things went all wrong for him, however, when Sirius escaped from Azkaban and tracked him down at Hogwarts. Along with Remus Lupin, he was about to kill Peter for his treachery when Harry intervened and stopped it—not out of pity for Peter, but because he didn't want Sirius and Remus to make themselves murderers just to avenge James's death. Harry intended that Wormtail should be sent to Azkaban, but instead he escaped back to Voldemort, but with his new debt as an unforeseen (and presumably unmentioned) burden [POA, p. 381].

In order to understand how Peter's life debt will play out in Book 7, we need to understand Peter himself. We learn almost nothing new about him in the last two books, however; it is from POA and GOF that we get most of our facts. As things stand at the end of HBP, Peter has turned up, contracted his life debt, taken part in Voldemort's rebirthing ceremony, and disappeared without a trace. (We're ignoring his stint as Scabbers here, because it tells us next to nothing about Peter himself.) Based on what we know about him up to this point, what is Peter really like?

Under the Fur: The Real Rat

Everything we know about Wormtail so far gives us clues to how his life debt will lead him to behave in Book 7. He is weak, cowardly, selfish, surly, and resentful; he seeks out the most powerful people he can find and tries to bask in their reflected glory and take advantage of their protection. Having done so, he spends his time figuring out how he can turn their power to his own advantage.

At school, he somehow managed to worm his way into James's and Sirius's gang, the Marauders. In it he played the part of the adoring idiot, hero-worshipping both James and Sirius, making appreciative noises at all the right times, and laughing at their jokes [OOTP, pp. 644-45]. This kept him going until they graduated, when he followed them into the Order of the Phoenix. And there Voldemort picked him off with ease.

Of course, Peter was being threatened by the Dark Lord, and he was terrified; but still, his behavior was inexcusable. He knew that his information would lead James and Lily to be murdered, and surely he would have assumed that the baby Harry would die as well, but he prized his own skin more highly than the lives of his friends. It is also clear that he did what he did partly for his own gain. After all, he was in the Order of the Phoenix, under the guard of none other than Albus Dumbledore, and yet he chose to side with the less-powerful Voldemort. If he'd gone to Dumbledore the moment Voldemort threatened him, he would have been protected; end of story. But he took a different path because he saw more benefit in it for himself. He saw an opportunity to be a part of the ruling Dark elite rather than just a mere soldier on the side of good.

Therefore, when Voldemort first threatened him, his actions in passing on Order information were triggered by pure cowardice. However, by the time he betrayed the Potters he had seen the advantages in working for the Dark side, and what he did then was driven by greed. Peter went from seeking out the powerful in order to look good himself, to organizing the murder of his own friends for gain, and he did so pretty quickly.

Voldemort himself knows how unreliable the affections of Wormtail are: "Your devotion is nothing more than cowardice. You would not be here if you had anywhere else to go" [GOF, p. 9]. As such, he treats Peter with the contempt that he deserves, making his life a misery. But Peter does get something he wants out of the arrangement. He has no self-respect, but he does have reflected glory, and he does have the ear of the most powerful wizard in the world to make him feel important.

Peter still does things only for his own gain; it's just that he has little choice left anymore. Voldemort doesn't trust him, and for this reason he does his best not to let Peter in on anything important. To the Dark Lord, Wormtail's usefulness ended when he cut off his hand to add to the regeneration potion [GOF, p. 641], and now he is just a liability.

Peter, however, is cleverer than he is often made out to be. He did, after all, master the exceptionally difficult animagus transformation, with a little help from his friends [POA, p. 354]. He also performed a faultless Avada Kedavra on Cedric Diggory with some-one else's wand [GOF, p. 638]. Avada Kedavra is a complex spell that requires "a powerful bit of magic behind it" [GOF, p. 217], and to per-form it so well with the wrong wand is the work of a very competent wizard.

This clever streak makes him dangerous—but dangerous to his master, not to anyone else. Voldemort has tried to get rid of him by banishing him to be Snape's house servant [HBP, p. 23]. But Peter is still there, watching, listening at doors, and trying to pick up on anything that he can use to his own advantage.

It will be no surprise to Voldemort when Peter turns against him in Book 7, for Voldemort never believed he was loyal in the first place. At first, he won't care, either: Peter is dispensable. But Volde-mort will change his mind when he sees how much damage Wormtail is able to do with his pieced-together knowledge. The discovery will take him aback, because Peter will do the unthinkable—he will save the life of the boy he once tried to condemn to death.

But the one man who will be most surprised by Peter's sudden urge to help Harry will be none other than Peter himself. He won't be intending to help him because he never does anything unselfish. But he will find himself bound by the impenetrable magic of the life debt. And so, without knowing why, he will save Harry anyway. The Worm is about to turn!

How Will Wormtail Pay Off His Debt?

Now that Dumbledore is dead, Peter has already started to feel braver. His master's worst enemy is gone, and all that remains is to kill Harry Potter. What could be easier? Peter sees his dearest wish coming true—to get the glory without any risk. As Book 7 opens, he will stop skulking around in the background; he'll gain a taste for more action. He thinks he'll be able to show how useful he can be to the cause without actually putting himself in the line of danger.

Voldemort will see this as an opportunity: He can use Peter as cannon fodder. If Peter does something helpful, all well and good;

if he dies, no loss. What Voldemort hasn't considered is that Peter could do serious damage to his cause because Voldemort has always underestimated Peter's intelligence. We believe this mistake will cost Voldemort his victory in the end. That might sound overdramatic, but the truth is that when Wormtail is around, disaster is always just around the corner. You only have to see the way that he let Bartemius Crouch Sr. escape when he was meant to be guarding him [GOF, p. 689], or look at what happened when the Potters trusted him to be their Secret Keeper [POA, pp. 365 & 369] to recognize that.

Feeling safe in the company of Voldemort and Snape, Wormtail will talk his way into Voldemort's inner circle. We may wonder why Voldemort would want him on the team, but remember that Wormtail is no idiot, and most of the Death Eaters are dead, or locked up in Azkaban. Bellatrix Lestrange will be detained by her own conflict with Neville Longbottom, and with quality supporters becoming a little hard to come by, even Wormtail is a better bet than someone as insane and unpredictable as Fenrir Greyback.

But keeping Peter around will have serious consequences for Voldemort. Peter knows too much. After all, he's always in the background, watching and listening for anything that might be useful to him. And surely, after all his time spent in Voldemort's company, he will have learned a thing or two about Horcruxes.

Assuming that Harry is a Horcrux, as discussed in Chapter 12, Peter's insider information will become extremely useful to Harry, who will be faced with a very unpleasant dilemma in Book 7: If Harry is a Horcrux, and all the Horcruxes must be destroyed to defeat Voldemort, doesn't it logically follow that Harry will have to destroy himself? We predict that Harry will be on the verge of killing himself when Wormtail will come to Harry's aid. Forced by the magic of the life debt, Wormtail will quite unwillingly describe to Harry how it is possible to destroy the Horcrux without destroying the vessel that holds it.

In doing so, he will save Harry's life and fulfill his life debt. But his reward will be most severe. Voldemort won't be happy with Peter for his treachery. And since Peter's usefulness was marginal at best to the Dark Lord before, it is quite likely that Voldemort will dispatch him with a cold and swift Killing Curse when he learns what Peter has done.

And so Peter's selfish life will come to an end, as he is cast aside and killed by the master he chose, because he has become a liability to him. What's more, he will be mourned by nobody, least of all by Voldemort.

Back when he was a child, Peter Pettigrew had the chance to be one of the good guys, a chance to be like his idols James and Sirius. But he let cowardice and greed lead him to the Dark side. He decided that his friends and their baby should be sacrificed for his own gain, but never earned the respect of his new master. And ironically, it will be that master who kills him in the end once he has no further use for him. Wormtail was unloved, and in death will be unmissed. His life debt, however, did lead him—against his will—to prevent Harry from killing himself, and for that he will always be a part of the final defeat of the Dark Lord.

R.A.B. and the Missing Locket

As readers all over the world turned the final page in *Harry Potter and the Half-Blood Prince*, not even the shock of Dumbledore's death or Snape's supposed betrayal could distract them from the enigma that is R.A.B. Who is R.A.B.? How did he or she know about Voldemort's Horcruxes? Why did R.A.B. want to destroy the Horcruxes? Who helped R.A.B. steal the locket Horcrux? Assuming that R.A.B is dead, how did he or she die? Was R.A.B. one of the good guys? These are a few of the questions that we will strive to answer in this chapter.

Who Is R.A.B?

Like Harry, we were crushed to discover that the Horcrux Dumbledore had retrieved from the cave at the cost of his life was a fake [HBP, p. 609]. If Dumbledore died to find a Horcrux that had already been found, then Dumbledore died for nothing. Right?

Wrong. Dumbledore did not die for nothing—mainly because a seemingly small shred of information came folded up inside the locket. The locket Dumbledore and Harry retrieved from the cave had been left in place of one of Voldemort's real Horcruxes (a locket that had belonged to Salazar Slytherin) and it contained the following message:

> To the Dark Lord
>
> *I know I will be dead long before you read this but I want you to know that it was I who discovered your secret. I have stolen the real Horcrux and intend to destroy it as soon as I can. I face death in the hope that when you meet your match, you will be mortal once more.*
>
> —*R.A.B.* [HBP, p. 609]

This message holds the key to the place where Harry's journey in Book 7 will begin.

With eager readers not far behind her, Hermione begins looking up the names of famous wizards with the initials R.A.B.: "Rosalind Antigone Bungs...Rupert 'Axebanger' Brookstanton...but they don't seem to fit at all" [HBP, p. 636].

Hermione is correct; these names don't fit at all, mainly because R.A.B. isn't going to be a character we've never heard of before. It is not in J.K.R.'s nature to introduce important characters or crucial plot points without foreshadowing them in previous books. Many characters in the series receive brief mentions before their roles become significant. Sirius Black is introduced in SS [SS, p. 14], but he doesn't become a central character until POA. Luna Lovegood's family is mentioned in GOF [GOF, p.73], but Luna doesn't become important to the plot until OOTP. Even Broderick Bode, the Unspeakable who is murdered in OOTP, is first mentioned briefly in GOF [GOF, p. 86]. Mrs. Figg is introduced as Harry's crazy old neighbor [SS, p. 22] long before we realize that she is a squib working under Dumbledore's orders to keep an eye on Harry [OOTP, pp. 20-21].

Moreover, Scabbers the rat is featured in both SS and COS, long before readers discover that he is actually an Animagus and Death Eater named Peter Pettigrew. These are just a few of many examples within the series, but they prove our point rather nicely; it's simply not like J.K.R. to introduce central characters in Book 7 who weren't at least mentioned in an earlier book. For this reason, we believe that R.A.B. is someone we've either seen or heard about in one of the first six books.

R.A.B. must also be someone who is or was closely connected to Voldemort. In saying, "I want you to know that it was I who discovered your secret," R.A.B. is demonstrating that connection, and suggesting that Voldemort will know who he or she is by the initials alone. Hermione admits that none of the people she's researched has had any known ties to Voldemort:

> *"Judging by that note, the person who stole the Horcrux knew Voldemort, and I can't find a shred of evidence that Bungs or Axebanger ever had anything to do with him…"* [HBP, p. 636]

Taking into consideration the matching initials, the foreshadowing in an earlier book, and the connection with Voldemort, who is the likeliest candidate?

Regulus Black.

Why Regulus Black? Regulus is first mentioned briefly in OOTP by his brother, Sirius [OOTP, pp. 111-12]. Apart from the obvious correlation between his name and the initials R.A.B., there is Regulus's history to consider. Regulus was a known Death Eater. According to Sirius, Regulus was "soft enough to believe" their parents' "pure-blood mania" [OOTP, p. 111], and joined the Death Eaters as a result [OOTP, pp. 111-12]. We do not know whether Sirius's assumption that Regulus shared their parents' "mania" is accurate. Whatever Regulus's reasons were for joining Voldemort, however, there is no doubt that he was employed in Voldemort's service for a short while. Regulus has the connection to Voldemort that others with the initials R.A.B. seem to lack.

What else is known about Regulus Black? Unfortunately, very little. We are told that Regulus died some fifteen years ago, around the same time Voldemort killed the Potters [OOTP, p. 112]. Sirius tells Harry that Regulus was a coward, killed when he decided that he no longer wanted to serve Voldemort and tried to back out of being a Death Eater:

> *"From what I found out after [Regulus] died, he got in so far, then panicked about what he was being asked to do and tried to back out. Well, you don't just hand in your resignation to Voldemort. It's a lifetime of service or death."* [OOTP, p. 112]

It's our belief that Sirius didn't know as much about his younger brother as he thought he did. The two weren't exactly close, so it is entirely probable that Sirius did not know the details of his brother's life and death. We will explore some of those possible details here.

How Did He Know about the Horcruxes?

How did R.A.B. know about the Horcruxes? This is a very good question, one that has not yet been answered in the series. Sirius assumes that Regulus "got in so far" before he panicked [OOTP, p. 112]. This is a very general statement. It does not tell us whether Regulus got into Voldemort's inner circle, or, if he did, how close he was to Voldemort. According to Dumbledore, Voldemort kept his Horcruxes a secret [HBP, p. 569]. We know, however, that Voldemort gave one of his Horcruxes, the diary of Tom Riddle, to Lucius Malfoy shortly before his first downfall [HBP, p. 508]. This happened roughly around the time that Regulus died. We do not have an exact date for either event, but it is possible that Regulus knew about the diary and knew that Voldemort had entrusted it to Lucius.

If Regulus, like Lucius, was a member of Voldemort's inner circle, it is not impossible that he was aware of the diary. The problem, of course, is that while Voldemort trusted Lucius with his Horcrux, he didn't trust Lucius far enough to tell him what it was. Voldemort never told Lucius that the diary held a piece of his soul—only that it was a powerfully enchanted object that could be used to open the Chamber of Secrets [HBP, p. 508]. If Lucius didn't know what the diary was, how could Regulus know? There is always the possibility that Regulus could have put two and two together, although this would imply that he knew something about Horcruxes in the first place. This is pure speculation, of course, but in the absence of hard fact, it provides a potential answer to the question of how R.A.B. knew about Voldemort's Horcruxes. How he could have learned that there was more than one Horcrux, if indeed he did know, is anyone's guess. And it is anyone's guess how Regulus knew about the cave, and how he knew that the Horcrux hidden in the cave was a locket. He must have known this beforehand, or he wouldn't have known to bring along a fake locket to leave behind as a decoy.

Why Did He Want to Steal Them?

Again, this is pure conjecture. If Sirius is right when he says that Regulus "got in so far, then panicked about what he was being asked to do" [OOTP, p. 112], it is possible that Regulus had a change of heart after he joined the Death Eaters. We know that Regulus was roughly eighteen years old when he was murdered. This means that he was barely of age when he joined the Death Eaters. Like Draco Malfoy, Regulus may simply have been an idealistic kid, enticed to join the Death Eaters by his family's pure-blood mania and the promise of power that Voldemort stood for, but with little idea of what being a Death Eater actually meant. And like Draco, Regulus may have learned that serving the Dark Lord was not as glamorous as he had thought.

Perhaps Regulus was more like his older brother than anyone realized—a foolishly daring young man with a flair for justice. It is possible that he did penetrate too far into Voldemort's service and was deeply shocked by what he found. But instead of panicking as Sirius assumes, he may have formed quite a different plan of action. If he was really repulsed by what he witnessed in Voldemort's service, Regulus may have decided not to run—at least not initially, and certainly not out of fear. He may have remained in Voldemort's service longer than he wanted to in the hope that he could somehow disrupt Voldemort's plans and stop the atrocities that so disgusted him. This would certainly seem to be consistent with the message that was left in the fake locket.

The message suggests that R.A.B. realized that he himself couldn't stop Voldemort. He just wanted to hurt Voldemort enough to enable the Chosen One to defeat him eventually. If Regulus left this note, as we believe he did, then Regulus wanted to taunt his former master with the knowledge that one of his own had turned against him. Regulus wanted to stay in Voldemort's service just long enough to find one of Voldemort's Horcruxes and destroy it, realizing that he would probably not live long after doing so. This means that he did not flee the Death Eaters out of fear; rather, he left them with a purpose. We don't know how Regulus learned where the locket Horcrux was hidden. What we do know, if the note can be used as evidence, is that Regulus hoped not so much to defeat Voldemort as to make it possible for someone else to defeat him. This is why he wanted to steal, and ultimately to destroy, the locket Horcrux.

This also explains why Sirius was unable to find more information about Regulus. If Regulus wanted to steal one of Voldemort's Horcruxes, he wouldn't have told anyone about his plans. Many of the Death Eaters seem to have been just as bloodthirsty as Voldemort himself, so it would not have been wise to confide in any of them. Regulus and Sirius were estranged and supposedly working for opposite sides of the war, so Regulus would have had neither the motive nor the opportunity to tell Sirius what he was up to. Regulus would have had to keep his plan to steal locket to himself.

But this raises a new question. If Regulus couldn't tell anyone that he planned to steal the locket, and if two people were needed to retrieve it, who helped Regulus to steal the locket Horcrux from the cave?

Who Helped Him to Steal the Locket?

We know that it took two people to steal the locket Horcrux. The locket was hidden at the bottom of a basin, on an island in the middle of a black lake, deep within a cave. The basin was filled with a poisonous green potion. One person must drink the entire potion to drain the basin and reach the locket. But having drunk the potion, this person would be rendered too weak to pick up the locket and escape. A second person was required to take the locket, cross back over the lake (which was full of Inferi), and get out of the cave alive [HBP, pp. 567-77]. Dumbledore remarks that this security system was "well-designed," since "one alone could not have [retrieved the locket]" [HBP, p. 577]. Voldemort tried to make it impossible for two people to reach the island at the same time by putting a spell on the boat that crossed the lake "so that only one wizard at a time will be able to sail in it" [HBP, p. 564].

But Voldemort made one mistake in designing his protective spell. He took into consideration only "the amount of magical power that crossed the lake" and not the actual number of people [HBP, p. 564]. As Dumbledore tells Harry before they enter the boat:

> *"I do not think you will count, Harry: You are underage and unqualified. Voldemort would never have expected a sixteen-year-old to reach this place: I think it unlikely that your powers will register compared to mine."* [HBP, p. 564]

The boat will hold two people, provided that only one of them is a powerful wizard. This proves that Regulus, like Dumbledore, would have been able to take an accomplice with him to the island. We don't know how much magical power Regulus had; we only know that he wasn't much older than Harry when he crossed the lake in Voldemort's little boat. Perhaps the boat didn't count Regulus, just as it didn't count Harry. This means that Regulus could have taken a powerful wizard with him to collect the Horcrux. He could have—but we know he didn't, because he couldn't tell anyone about his plans. So whom did Regulus take? Who better than a creature who was magically bound to obey his every command? Kreacher, the Black family's house-elf, accompanied Regulus to the island in the cave and helped him to steal Voldemort's Horcrux.

There are two possible scenarios that explain how Regulus and Kreacher could have retrieved the Horcrux. In the first scenario, Regulus drinks the green potion and has Kreacher help him steal the real Horcrux and leave the fake Horcrux in its place. In the second scenario, Regulus forces Kreacher to drink the potion. The potion must be poisonous to humans, because it was slowly killing Dumbledore, but it might not have been poisonous to Kreacher, who is not human. Some substances are known to affect house-elves differently than humans. For example, humans have little to no reaction to the small amount of alcohol present in butterbeer. House-elves, however, have a strong reaction to butterbeer; a small amount makes them highly intoxicated [GOF, p. 536]. The potion may account for Kreacher's deranged nature, but if he did drink the potion, it obviously didn't kill him. Either way, we think Harry's going to have a long list of questions for Kreacher in Book 7. Because Kreacher has now passed into Harry's ownership, he will be forced to answer those questions honestly. High up on the list will probably be the question of what really happened to Regulus.

Where Is the Locket Now?

If Regulus, with the help of Kreacher, took the locket Horcrux, where is it now? It is almost certain that the locket was taken to Grimmauld Place. After that, it is likely that one of two things happened.

In OOTP, Harry and his friends find a "heavy locket that none of them could open" while cleaning Grimmauld Place [OOTP, p. 116]. We believe this is the locket Horcrux that Regulus stole from the cave. We believe that Regulus was unable to destroy the Horcrux before he died, and that is why no one can open the locket. Grimmauld Place is a good hiding place, and it makes sense that Regulus would bring (or give Kreacher instructions to bring) the Horcrux there. Regulus's father put "every security measure known to Wizard-kind" [OOTP, p. 115] on Grimmauld Place to make it Unplottable, so what better place to hide the true locket Horcrux?

Where is it now? In the first scenario, it is still in Grimmauld Place. Kreacher has a habit of sneaking small Black family objects off to his sleeping quarters so that they cannot be thrown away [OOTP, pp. 109-10]. He is seen entering the very room where the heavy locket is found directly before it is mentioned [OOTP, p. 107]. It is therefore entirely possible that the locket is now lying forgotten in Kreacher's sleeping quarters.

In the second scenario, the locket has been removed from Grimmauld Place. Mundungus Fletcher has taken to stealing things from Grimmauld Place and selling them. Harry catches him in the act in HBP [pp. 245-46]. It is entirely probable that Mundungus has stolen the locket, not realizing its significance, and sold it. A one-time possession of Salazar Slytherin's, the locket would bring a good price if offered to the right person. If this is what happened to the locket Horcrux, it could be virtually anywhere, making Harry's search all the more difficult. Either of these scenarios would explain where the locket Horcrux is now. Only the final book will say for sure.

How Did R.A.B. Die?

Sirius says that Regulus "was murdered by Voldemort. Or on Voldemort's orders, more likely" [OOTP, p. 112]. If this is true, Regulus was not murdered for what would seem to be the obvious reason. At the time he died, Voldemort did not yet know that someone had stolen one of his Horcruxes. It follows that Voldemort could not have known that Regulus had stolen it. Regulus may have been murdered on Voldemort's orders for some other reason connected to the Horcrux, but not as a punishment for stealing the Horcrux. If Regulus did not return to Voldemort after stealing the Horcrux, Voldemort and the Death Eaters may have assumed that he merely ran away out of fear. If he was killed on Voldemort's orders, then, it was not because Voldemort knew that Regulus had the locket.

The note addressed "To the Dark Lord" states that the author knows that he "will be dead" long before Voldemort reads it [HBP, p. 609]. Assuming that R.A.B. is Regulus, this could mean one of three things:

1. Regulus drank the green potion and realized that it was going to kill him soon.
2. Regulus forced Kreacher to drink the green potion, so he himself was not poisoned, but he knew that he was going to be murdered shortly for reasons connected to his involvement with Voldemort.
3. Regulus forced Kreacher to drink the green potion, avoiding the poison himself, but he wrote the line about being dead soon to throw Voldemort off the scent. If this is the case, he could still be alive and hiding out somewhere.

Our bet is that Regulus is dead, either killed by the green potion or murdered by one of the Death Eaters for his supposed cowardice. If Regulus left the Death Eaters directly before or after stealing the locket, it was only a few days before he was killed. Lupin remarks on the quickness with which Regulus was murdered when he says:

"...well, frankly, I'm surprised he [Igor Karkaroff] stayed alive for even a year after deserting the Death Eaters; Sirius's brother, Regulus, only managed a few days as far as I can remember." [HBP, p. 106]

Why Regulus was killed so quickly we don't know; this question has gone unanswered so far in the series. Nor do we know why the other Death Eaters were so anxious to be rid of Regulus when it took them a year to track down Karkaroff. Did Regulus not go into hiding as Karkaroff did? If not, why not? Surely, if Regulus was smart enough to figure out that Voldemort was creating Horcruxes, where one Horcrux was located, and how to retrieve it, he was smart enough to know that he would be safest on the run. There are many questions surrounding both Regulus's time as a Death Eater and his premature death. We can only hope that Book 7 answers them all.

Good Guy or Bad Guy?

Just as Snape's allegiance to Voldemort is suspicious (more about that in Chapter 10), we think there is something odd about Regulus's position as a Death Eater. It's entirely possible that he was a genuine Death Eater once, but we think something must have made him change his mind. If we are right about Regulus, he is a good guy. At least, a fairly good guy. As the old saying goes, the enemy of my enemy is my friend, so anyone who has a beef with Voldemort is an ally of Harry's at this point.

Unfortunately for Harry, Regulus Black is almost certainly dead. But if by some slim chance he is alive, we expect that Harry will look to him for help in locating the last of the Horcruxes. On the off chance that Regulus has been faking his death all these years, he should have some good advice for Harry. However, we think that it will be Kreacher who provides Harry with the answers he needs. One thing we think Harry is sure to learn in Book 7 is that there is no defining line between good people and Death Eaters. Or, as Sirius puts it, "the world isn't split into good people and Death Eaters" [OOTP, p. 302]. We think one thing Harry is going to discover is that there are many shades of gray in the wizarding world.

Snape

Severus Snape is a dark and complex character, an exciting mix of the good, the bad, and the mysterious. One minute he's going out of his way to save Harry's life during a Quidditch match [SS, p. 190], and the next he's sneering at him with all his might. He's been a Death Eater in the past, and for all we know, he could still be one right now. He used every ounce of skill he had to heal Dumbledore when he was injured by the ring Horcrux [HBP, p. 503], but later he murdered him. Just what is going on in that twisted mind of his? And above all, whose side is he really on?

One thing is certain: Severus Snape is, on the surface, an unpleasant man. As a teacher, he delights in bullying students he's taken a dislike to, and in blatantly favoring students from his own house (Slytherin). He is petty, he is vindictive, and he can bear a grudge for years. He is universally disliked (except by Slytherin students), mainly because he is so fundamentally unlikable.

On the other hand, Snape is a brilliant wizard. He's a fantastic Occlumens and Legilimens, and Albus Dumbledore, the greatest wizard of the age, trusted him to the end. He is also the only person ever to have defected from the ranks of the Death Eaters [GOF, p. 590] and lived to tell about it—if in fact he did defect. More about that later.

But then, at the climax of HBP, he kills Dumbledore. So whose side is he really on?

J.K.R. has undoubtedly set Snape up to be a mystery. There are frequent contradictions and a huge number of red herrings whenever he appears throughout the series. But if you look at it carefully enough, you always arrive at the same place: Snape is one of the good guys. He may not be nice, and he may have revoltingly greasy hair, but he is on the side of good and always will be.

Snape's Double Life

A lot of people believe that J.K.R. thoroughly debunked the "Snape is good" theory in the MuggleNet/Leaky Cauldron interview (July 2005). If you look at it carefully, though, you'll see that all J.K.R. does is avoid the question, which tells us nothing (apart from the fact that it's important and she doesn't want to talk about it). What was said was this:

> **MA:** *OK, big big big book six question. Is Snape evil?*
>
> **J.K.R.:** *Harry-Snape is now as personal, if not more so, than Harry-Voldemort. I can't answer that question because it's a spoiler, isn't it, whatever I say, and obviously, it has such a huge impact on what will happen when they meet again that I can't. And let's face it, it's going to launch 10,000 theories and I'm going to get a big kick out of reading them so [laughs]. I'm evil but I just like the theories, I love the theories.*

Is that really someone confidently debunking a theory? It most certainly is not! Put simply, this answer falls well short of providing the cold, hard facts we want.

HOW OLD IS SNAPE?

Severus Snape was born on January 9, 1959, to the Muggle Tobias Snape and the witch Eileen Prince. Most sources put his birth in 1960, but the available information disproves this. J.K.R. stated in the Comic Relief interview from 2001 (after the publication of GOF but before OOTP) that Snape was 35 or 36 years of age, meaning that he must have been born in 1959 or 1960. But the scene shown in Snape's Worst Memory [OOTP, pp. 645-49] is described as having occurred "over 20 years ago," and Harry is seeing it in 1996. The scene took place in Snape's fifth year at Hogwarts, which therefore must have been 1975 at the latest. Combined, these two pieces of information set his year of birth as 1959.

The important thing to remember about Snape is that he is a double agent for one side or the other. He's either playing Voldemort or he's playing Dumbledore. He still has to perform his duties and appear to be loyal to whomever he is deceiving, however, in order to avoid being suspected. How, then, can we judge which side he is really on? By looking at the things he does that he didn't have to do in order to maintain his cover.

A popular theory is that Snape is just out for himself, keeping in with both sides so that he will be in the right place whoever wins. This, however, simply can't be true. Taking an Unbreakable Vow [HBP, pp. 36-37] and killing Dumbledore [HBP, p. 596] hardly qualify as keeping in with both sides. If this is what he is trying to do, he fails miserably. Whatever you think of him, Snape is no idiot; if he wanted to stay in with everyone, he could do better than that. So the "Snape is out for himself" theory goes into the trash, and we are left with a straight fight between Good and Evil.

Snape and Lily

When Severus Snape entered Hogwarts, he was a social inadequate looking for friends. The flashes into his childhood that Harry sees when he is taking Occlumency lessons [OOTP, p. 592] show that Severus was an awkward and unpopular boy. This is reaffirmed in the memory of Snape's that Harry sees in the Pensieve. Even though James Potter was clearly bullying Snape, the other students saw it as entertainment:

> *Several people watching laughed; Snape was clearly*
> *unpopular.* [OOTP, p. 646]

Snape's home life as a child was unhappy [OOTP, p. 592], and he may have thought that by going to Hogwarts he was escaping, but he was wrong: He just went from one wretched life to another. There was one person at the school who was sympathetic to him, though, one person who dared to stand up to James and his gang, one person who dared not to laugh even when the rest of the school was laughing. Her name was Lily Evans:

> *"Leave him alone," Lily repeated. She was looking at James*
> *with every sign of great dislike. "What's he done to you?"*
> [OOTP, p. 647]

There is no evidence that they were friends in the traditional sense, but this episode from "Snape's Worst Memory" shows how she stood up for him when nobody else would. It is easy to infer from this that she would also have been kind to him at other times, and that she would have been happy enough to be friendly towards him.

Lily was popular, pretty, and vivacious, and people like Snape simply aren't used to that sort of girl being kind to them. It was only to be expected, then, that Snape would fall in love with her. Lily never intended this to happen, and she may not even have been aware that it was happening, but happen it did.

Some people try to refute the "Snape loves Lily" theory by saying that all Slytherins are pure-blood bigots. According to that logic, Snape, who seems to embody all things Slytherin, could never love Lily, since she was Muggle-born. This is simply not the case, however. True, most Slytherins are bigots—Draco and his father,

Pansy Parkinson, Blaise Zabini. But we've seen at least one example of a Slytherin who is not prejudiced against Muggles: Horace Slughorn. This is how Slughorn describes Lily, whom he taught when he was a Slytherin teacher at Hogwarts:

> *"You shouldn't have favorites as a teacher, of course, but she was one of mine. Your mother,"* Slughorn added, *in answer to Harry's questioning look. "Lily Evans. One of the brightest I ever taught. Vivacious, you know. Charming girl."* [HBP, pp. 69-70]

This clearly shows that not all Slytherins are prejudiced against Muggles, and it rules out the possibility that Snape, as a Slytherin, would automatically hate Lily for being Muggle-born. Another clue to Snape's lack of bigotry is the fact that Snape is a half-blood himself, the Half-Blood Prince, to be exact, and that he makes no attempt to hide it. But although this proves that Snape wouldn't dislike Lily just for being Muggle-born, it doesn't prove that he loved her.

Admittedly, there is not a lot of evidence to support this idea. There is one telling clue, however, in the "Snape's Worst Memory" episode that we've just been looking at. Most people think that Snape was particularly protective of this memory because of the humiliation of having his grimy underpants on display to the school. Snape, however, had been at war with James and Sirius for years [OOTP, p. 670], and Levicorpus—the spell used on him on this occasion—was very popular at the time. As Lupin says:

FUN WITH SNAPE

Here's a fun Snape tidbit: If you rearrange "Severus Snape" you get "persues Evans." You really shouldn't take this anagram seriously, though—it's just a coincidence, and you even have to misspell the word "pursues" to make it work! In other words, forget the anagrams; they're fun but they don't mean a thing.

"There were a few months in my fifth year when you couldn't move for being hoisted into the air by your ankle." [HBP, p. 336]

By this, Lupin means that during the months in question, everybody was at risk of being lifted into the air at any moment, and the implication is that Snape was targeted just as much as everyone else—probably more so, considering his unpopularity. Bearing this in mind, surely James did much worse to Snape at other times, and this particular incident was run-of-the-mill.

Furthermore, Snape is a grown man now and a powerful wizard, locked in a battle to the death with either Dumbledore or Voldemort, the two strongest wizards alive. So dirty underwear is probably not the first thing on his mind. The real reason Snape hides this memory is because he is ashamed of what he said to James when she tried to help him:

"I don't need help from filthy little Mudbloods like her!"
[OOTP, p. 648]

Snape was mortified that she had seen him so vulnerable, so he lashed out against her with these hurtful words even though he didn't mean them. And in doing so, he drove away the one person who had ever showed any genuine kindness to him. The fact that Snape hides this memory in the Pensieve clearly shows the depth of his feelings for Lily. Remember: There were only three memories hidden in the Pensieve, and if Snape truly didn't care deeply about Lily, why would this memory be one of them? We've already proved that it wasn't because of his humiliation at the hands of James and Sirius. That leaves only one other option: Snape loved Lily, and he was deeply ashamed that he drove her away with his own cruelty.

Right now, "Did Snape love Lily?" is one of the big questions that everyone wants an answer to. J.K.R. is going to have to satisfy that curiosity one way or another come Book 7. And when she does, rest assured that there will be a lot of people gasping, "Oh my God!"

Snape and Lucius

Snape's lack of friends and social skills not only made him a target for the bullies, but also made him easy prey for someone else—someone who wanted something quite different. That someone was Lucius Malfoy. We learn in HBP that Snape is an old school friend of Lucius. At first glance, this is no surprise, since they are both Slytherins and both either former or current Death Eaters. However, Lucius is five years older than Severus, which makes their boyhood friendship a little unlikely. So how did it happen?

We already know from Sirius that Snape's knowledge of curses was remarkable even before he reached Hogwarts [GOF, p. 531], and nobody disputes the fact that Snape had an intense interest in the Dark Arts. He was just the sort of person that Lucius needed: brilliant but socially inept, and therefore malleable. Snape was eager for acceptance and, in his vulnerable state, it seems likely that he would have joined any group that would have him. And so Snape became part of a gang who, according to Sirius, nearly all went on to become Death Eaters [GOF, p. 531].

The amused reaction of the rest of the school when James bullied Snape makes it clear that the members of this gang were his only friends, and it would have taken a much more resilient boy than Snape not to hang on to them for all he was worth. As we have shown, Snape is no pure-blood bigot, yet by his fifth year he is shouting abuse at the Muggle-born girl he loves in a way that would have made Lucius proud.

The implication is clear. Snape played the part of the pure-blood bigot to keep himself in with the gang. When Lily tried to save him from James, he was angry and humiliated. He spoke with an attitude drummed into him by his Slytherin colleagues, and it cost him her friendship. She was the one good, kind thing in his life, and he drove her away. More than this, the moment when he drove her away was also the moment that sealed his destiny to become a Death Eater. He had no other friends, no one else to follow, so he did what was necessary to still belong. His friends joined the ranks of the Death Eaters, and so did he.

A Genuine Defection?

While he was a Death Eater, Snape overheard half of Sybill Trelawney's prophecy about the birth of a boy who had the power to defeat the Dark Lord:

> *The one with the power to vanquish the Dark Lord*
> *approaches....Born to those who have thrice defied him,*
> *Born as the seventh month dies...* [OOTP, p. 841]

He reported that prophecy straight back to Voldemort. This made him very popular with his master, but it also set into motion the events that led to his defection.

But was his change of heart genuine? Or was he really just spying on Dumbledore, as Voldemort thought he was?

The problem for Snape was that having heard the half-prophecy, Voldemort worked out that the boy he had to kill was none other than Harry Potter, the young son of James Potter and Lily Evans. Not only was Snape about to become responsible for Lily's murder, he was also bound by a life debt to James.

Here's how it happened. Sirius, who was always more reckless than James, decided one day to play a potentially fatal prank on Snape, which in his view would have "served him right" for daring to be at war with them [POA, p. 356]. The joke in question was to tell Snape how to immobilize the Whomping Willow in the school grounds, so he could get past it and find out what lay beyond. But what lay beyond was in fact a full-grown werewolf (the transformed Remus Lupin), who would have killed Snape the instant he saw him. When James heard what Sirius had done, he went after Snape, at great risk to himself, and pulled him back, thus saving his life [POA, p. 357].

You can read about life debts in more detail in Chapter 8. Here it is sufficient to say that when one wizard saves the life of another, it creates a strong magical bond between the two, forcing the saved wizard to do everything in his power to return the favor [POA, p. 427].

And so, when he realized whom Voldemort had targeted, Snape did what he had to do: He defected from the Death Eaters [GOF, p. 590]. His feelings for Lily and the life debt are proof enough that his change of heart was genuine. But there is another reason to believe that Snape was sincere. Dumbledore trusted him.

Why Did Dumbledore Trust Snape?

Dumbledore had always been absolutely convinced that Snape's defection from the Death Eaters was genuine. His reasons for trusting Snape are a closely guarded secret, however, one to which J.K.R. has provided no clues. Nobody—not even the other members of the Order—knows why. Dumbledore even kept his reasons secret from the Hogwarts teachers, including Minerva McGonagall [HBP, p. 616].

"That, Harry, is a matter between Professor Snape and myself" is all that Dumbledore had to say on the matter when pressed [GOF, p. 604]. Now that he's dead, we are unlikely to hear any more from him about it.

While there is no hard evidence on this subject, we have what we think is a likely explanation. Having been the Headmaster when Snape was a boy at school, Dumbledore would probably have known about his feelings for Lily, and about his debt to James. He therefore could have concluded that Snape's change of heart was genuine and binding. As Snape himself says, he told Dumbledore a tale of deep remorse [HBP, p. 31], and Dumbledore believed him. But it's worth noting that Dumbledore didn't immediately take his

RISING STAR

Snape's new role as a spy shows that his powers were incredible even at the age of 21. His Occlumency was already strong enough to withstand Voldemort, who is believed by his admirers to be the greatest Legilimens the world has ever seen [HBP, p. 26]. And not only could he hide his true thoughts, he could do so without Voldemort suspecting that anything was being hidden. Snape was becoming, behind Dumbledore and Voldemort, the third most powerful wizard in the world.

words at face value, since Snape had not yet proved his loyalty. Dumbledore therefore made Snape take an Unbreakable Vow binding him to the Order of the Phoenix.

This is not the last time Snape takes an Unbreakable Vow, however. He also takes one with Narcissa Malfoy that compels him to help Draco kill Dumbledore [HBP, pp. 36-37]. These two Vows are clearly contradictory; he can hardly serve the Order and kill Dumbledore, too. But if you break an Unbreakable Vow, you die; it's as simple as that [HBP, pp. 325-26]. And so in taking two contradictory Vows, Snape was voluntarily condemning himself to death. As it happens, later events were to save him (more about that later). In any case, by the time Snape starts as a teacher at Hogwarts, he has turned full circle—from Dark Arts–obsessed Death Eater to Order of the Phoenix spy. And Book 7 will explain exactly how he did it.

Does Snape Really Have It in for Harry?

In a word, yes and no. At school, Snape makes Harry's life a misery; he belittles him in front of the class at every opportunity and puts him in unnecessarily unpleasant detentions for the most minor of misdemeanors whenever he can. But while Snape is bullying Harry relentlessly, he is also doing everything he can to keep him safe from harm.

There are two reasons for this. First, as a loyal member of the Order, Snape is trying to protect Harry from Voldemort. Second, James and Lily's murder would have been very important to Snape. Their deaths meant that he had failed his life debt to James. Normally, this life debt would have ended with James's death. After all, the debt could no longer be fulfilled. But the debt is actually passed on in this case (in Snape's mind, if not magically) from James to Harry. Dumbledore made this clear when he explained to Harry why Snape had spent an entire year trying to save Harry from Professor Quirrell:

> *"Funny, the way people's minds work, isn't it? Professor*
> *Snape couldn't bear being in your father's debt....I do believe*
> *he worked so hard to protect you this year because he felt that*
> *would make him and your father even."* [SS, p. 300]

But there are other reasons that this debt is passed on, in addition to the fact that Snape "couldn't bear" being indebted to James. Snape felt especially guilty failing James in this instance because he didn't merely *fail* to save James, he actually helped to *cause* James's death. And as if that weren't bad enough, his actions led to the murder of Lily, the only girl he'd ever loved. And so Snape's intense guilt led to his passing on the debt in his mind from James to Harry. Having failed James, Snape is going to save Harry if it kills him!

Despite all this, Snape is set up as evil throughout SS, where he plays the role of a classic pantomime villain-who-isn't. Every scene finds him in a compromising position that suggests that he is up to no good, with false clues flying in all directions, while in fact he is battling Quirrell and saving Harry's life. This is particularly important because Snape contracts a life debt of his own when he saves Harry from being murdered by Quirrell during Harry's first game of Quidditch [SS, p. 190]. When he prevents Quirrell from making Harry fall to his death, he believes that he is fulfilling the life debt that he still owes to James. But none of the information we have about life debts suggests that they can be passed from father to son, and so he is actually creating a debt from Harry to himself. This new life debt will play a crucial role in Book 7.

The fact remains that Snape really doesn't treat Harry well at school. One thing that the "Snape is evil" camp often point out is that he keeps trying to get Harry expelled when he knows that without Dumbledore's protection, Harry would not last a day. However, if we read these expulsion threats carefully, we see that they are empty threats, designed to scare Harry; there is no chance that they will actually be carried out. Snape knows that Dumbledore would never allow Harry to be expelled, but he also wants to belittle him and make him a bit more obedient, so he threatens him. The one time Snape fears that Harry may really be expelled (for confronting Sirius in the Shrieking Shack), he actually defends him, even though Harry has just caused him to be thrown across the room and knocked unconscious [POA, p. 361].

In short, Snape's dealings with Harry during his time at Hogwarts show him to be exactly what he is: a brave and loyal member of the Order of the Phoenix, but a man with a chip the size of Belgium on his shoulder and a nasty streak a mile wide.

Memories

Snape's nasty streak is never more apparent than when he agrees to teach Occlumency to Harry [OOTP, p. 518]. During these lessons he bullies Harry even more than usual before he finally throws him out of his office. But before these lessons, he uses the Pensieve to hide some of his memories. That is very revealing, because out of all his memories, Snape chooses to conceal only three.

Snape knows that Harry may see his own memories during the lesson, so he takes the precaution of putting three of them in the Pensieve. One of them is the memory of his encounter with James and Sirius, and it is reasonable to assume that the other two are similar. This is supported by the fact that when Snape catches Harry, he knows that Harry is looking at a memory of James attacking him without needing to dip into the Pensieve himself. This means that Snape has nothing to hide regarding his dealings with Voldemort or the Dark Arts. If he were really working for the Dark Lord, he would have to conceal a vast number of secrets—memories of things that would blow his cover in an instant if he didn't keep them hidden. Yet he chooses not to hide any memories of his Dark activities (or if you want to push it, he hides a maximum of two of them). This implication is clear: Snape has little or nothing to hide.

Bellatrix's Question

Bellatrix Lestrange (quite sensibly, as it turns out) is skeptical about Snape's loyalty to the Dark Lord. Why, she asks, has he failed to kill Harry in the five years that he has been teaching him [HBP, p. 25]? She is quite right to ask, of course, and Snape's answer—basically, that he didn't feel like it—convinces nobody, least of all Bellatrix. In the end Snape has to take an Unbreakable Vow to kill Dumbledore in order to persuade her that he is true to Voldemort [HBP, pp. 36-37]. The real answer is that Snape hasn't killed Harry because he is not a loyal Death Eater and so doesn't want him dead, however much he hates him.

He has, in fact, made something of a habit of saving (or trying to save) Harry's life. The first time he did so was at the Quidditch game, in the incident cited above [SS, p. 190]. The second time was when he followed Harry to the Shrieking Shack to save him from Sirius, whom he mistakenly believed was about to murder Harry [POA, p. 359]. He also helped to rescue Harry from Bartemius Crouch Jr., when Crouch was about to kill him in Voldemort's name [GOF, p. 683]. (Note, by the way, that in this incident, Snape appears in Crouch's Foe-Glass, showing that they are not allies—proof that Snape is no longer a Death Eater.)

Finally, Snape speeds off into the Forbidden Forest to try to stop Harry from going to the Ministry when he realizes that Harry has fallen for Voldemort's mind trick and believes that Sirius has been kidnapped [OOTP, p. 731]. The entire Order knew that Voldemort was trying to get inside Harry's mind, and that if he succeeded, Harry could be killed, which was why they had insisted that he learn Occlumency [OOTP, p. 519]. Snape knows that Harry's life is in danger, and he does his utmost to try to save him.

In order to keep up the suspense, J.K.R. still does her best to keep the finger of suspicion pointing at Snape by reminding us of his past, having him constantly applying for the D.A.D.A. job, and having Ron Weasley try to associate him with whatever danger Harry is grappling with at the moment.

"But what if Snape was really doing x, y, and z?" he can often be heard to say.

What Snape has really been doing, however, in between teaching Harry and bullying him to make himself feel better, is working for the Order and trying to keep Harry safe. Bellatrix suspected it, but in the end she never thought Snape would take the Unbreakable Vow if he didn't mean it. So she missed the boat, and Snape's cover stayed intact.

The Forbidden Forest Episode

Snape's trek into the Forbidden Forest provides further convincing evidence of his loyalty. Harry dreams that he has seen Sirius being tortured at the Ministry by Voldemort. He rushes to Dolores Umbridge's office to try to contact Sirius via the Floo Network in order to find out if the dream is true [OOTP, p. 740]. Unfortunately, Umbridge catches him and traps him in her study. She summons Snape to help question him, and with every other Order member gone, Snape is Harry's last chance of communicating with the Order. He shouts at Snape in code (so as not to alert Umbridge), and Snape pretends not to understand, but immediately goes off to contact the Order himself. If he were just trying to keep his cover, he wouldn't have had to do this; no members of the Order were present, and if he'd done nothing nobody would have known. But instead he contacts the Order and then goes straight into the Forest to try to prevent Harry from going to the Ministry. The result is that the Order shows up at the Ministry to fight against the Death Eaters; Harry escapes; and the Prophecy is lost. Snape has foiled the Dark Lord's plan single handed—the prophecy that Voldemort so wants is lost forever, and most of his followers wind up in Azkaban. There is simply no way that a loyal Death Eater would have done it.

The Draco Plot

The plot to have Draco murder Dumbledore—Voldemort's plot—tells us a lot about Snape and which side he is on. The first issue is a very simple one: Dumbledore knows that Draco is trying to kill him. But how does he know?

There's only one way he could have found out, because Draco has learned enough Occlumency to deny even an advanced Legilimens access to his mind [HBP, p. 322]. Snape must have told him. He didn't have to do this; he could easily have pretended he didn't know. But he told Dumbledore every detail he knew of the Dark Lord's most secret and important plan.

And far from helping with the plot, Snape hinders it in every way he can. Look at what he does after Dumbledore destroys the ring Horcrux [HBP, p. 503]. Voldemort's real goal is to get rid of Dumbledore; he only wants to use Draco to get back at Lucius, and at this point he hasn't even given Draco the assignment. We can assume that he would be just as happy if Snape did the job. The Dark magic of the ring Horcrux was pretty nasty, and only Snape had the expertise to understand the curse that Voldemort had put on it. He could easily have pretended to try to save Dumbledore while actually doing nothing. Nobody would have been any the wiser. He would have received the full sympathy of the Hogwarts staff for trying his best; he could have stayed in his position in the Order and continued to spy on them; and he would have performed the task that Voldemort wanted, thereby cementing his position as the Dark Lord's most trusted follower. Instead, he chose to save Dumbledore's life and restore him to full health (except for the irreparable damage to his hand). These are not the actions of a loyal Death Eater posing as a member of the Order.

And if the Dark Lord were adamant that Draco should be the one to kill Dumbledore, Snape—if he were a loyal Death Eater—would pretend to try to save Dumbledore's life, leaving him as weak as possible to give Draco the best chance. But that's not what he does. He saves Dumbledore, a task that no Death Eater would have carried out.

The Murder

Snape does kill Dumbledore in the end, of course. At first sight this looks like proof that he is evil after all, but in fact, it is anything but. The most obvious part of this scene that raises suspicion is Dumbledore's begging:

> "*Severus... please...*" [HBP, p. 595]

A lot of people interpret this as a plea for Snape to spare his life. But is this even remotely likely? In a word, no. After all, Dumbledore is already facing Draco Malfoy and four Death Eaters, including the violently insane Fenrir Greyback, and he hasn't seen fit to beg for his life at any point. Why suddenly start begging when Snape turns up?

Dumbledore has never once doubted Snape's loyalty, and so, regardless of Snape's true intentions, what Dumbledore sees is his trusted friend and ally, arriving just in the nick of time. In these circumstances he would naturally do one of two things:

- If he thought the situation was hopeless, he would tell Snape to run and save himself.
- If he thought there was hope, he would expect Snape to make a heroic attempt to rescue him.

In neither case would he beg Snape for his life. Why would anybody beg his trusted friend not to murder him? And to top it all off, we know that Dumbledore doesn't fear death anyway—he just regards it as the next great adventure [SS, p. 297].

So we can only conclude that Dumbledore's cries mean something quite different. Dumbledore is begging Snape to abide by an agreement they had made at some point after Snape's meeting with Narcissa. The agreement was that, for the good of the cause and to protect the only chance they had of destroying Voldemort, Snape was to kill Dumbledore if necessary.

We know this because Hagrid overhears Snape and Dumbledore talking about it. Hagrid thinks Snape is just complaining about being overworked, and it's easy to see why. But what is really being discussed is something infinitely more sinister. This is how Hagrid reported what he heard:

> "...I jus' heard Snape sayin' Dumbledore took too much fer granted an' maybe he—Snape—didn' wan' ter do it anymore.... Dumbledore told him flat out he'd agreed ter do it an' that was all there was to it." [HBP, pp. 405-406]

The conversation isn't mentioned again in the book, so it's impossible to prove that Hagrid was actually overhearing the agreement being made. However, it is worth noting that Dumbledore and Snape *must* have made just such an agreement in order for Snape's seemingly contradictory Unbreakable Vows (one to serve the Order of the Phoenix and one to help Draco kill Dumbledore) to function simultaneously without killing Snape. Furthermore, J.K.R. never drops things like this into the plot without a purpose, and there is no reference anywhere else to Snape feeling overworked. The passage therefore has to be a clue to the agreement Dumbledore and Snape had between them.

The demand that Dumbledore makes of Snape is almost exactly the same demand that he makes of Harry when they go to the cave to retrieve the fake Horcrux [HBP, pp. 550-51]. There, he tells Harry to make him keep on drinking the emerald potion from the basin, even if it looks as if the potion will kill him. And Harry does it, although the hate and revulsion that he feels are almost too much for him to bear [HBP, p. 571].

The terms of his agreement with Dumbledore mean that Snape has very similar instructions. And so, when he finally has to kill him, Snape feels exactly the same emotions that Harry feels in the cave:

> *"Snape gazed for a moment at Dumbledore, and there was revulsion and hatred etched in the harsh lines of his face."*
> [HBP, p. 595]

Snape's emotions as he kills Dumbledore, and their similarity to what Harry feels as he pours the emerald potion into Dumbledore's mouth, show exactly which side Snape is on.

Snape doesn't like it, and when it comes to the point, Dumbledore isn't convinced that he will see it through. So he begs Snape to comply, and though he hates what he is doing, Snape doesn't shirk his responsibilities. He kills Dumbledore, and in that single moment he does the bravest thing that he has ever done.

After the Killing

But Snape hasn't finished being heroic just yet. He is still thinking about the mission to defeat Voldemort. With Dumbledore gone, he has some important information to pass on to Harry, and he is desperate to find a chance to speak to him. When Snape and Draco flee after the murder, they have a long head start, and Harry isn't even sure whether they have run to the Room of Requirement or the doors of the castle [HBP, p. 600]. Suddenly a bloody footprint appears to point him in the right direction, followed by a smear of blood on a flagstone. Is that a coincidence? Of course not. Snape planted both of those clues intentionally so that Harry could catch up with him.

When Harry finally does catch up with him, Snape takes the opportunity to pass on as many clues about how to fight Voldemort as he can (delivered in his usual contemptuous style), even though Harry is attempting to curse him every few seconds. He could blast Harry out of the way without a second thought if he wanted to, but instead he stands there and lectures him on the value of nonverbal spells and the importance of avoiding Unforgivable Curses. Why does he do that? Purely and simply, to improve Harry's chances of defeating the Dark Lord.

With the curses flying at him, Snape's restraint in the face of provocation, and his determination to pass on this information, are admirable. He even prevents his fellow Death Eaters from casting the Cruciatus Curse on Harry. He finally loses his temper, though, and understandably so, when Harry attempts to use Snape's own Sectumsempra and Levicorpus spells against him, and then calls Snape a coward:

> *"Kill me then," panted Harry.... "Kill me like you killed him, you coward—"*
>
> *"DON'T—" screamed Snape, and his face was suddenly demented, inhuman, as though he was in as much pain as the yelping, howling dog stuck in the burning house behind them, "—CALL ME COWARD!"* [HBP, p. 604]

After all, Snape has just thrown his life away for the cause. The very last thing he could be is a coward. Knowing what he has done, he is enraged by Harry's taunts, and on top of that, Harry's choice of spells reminds him of his humiliation by James and the loss of Lily. Even then, however, rather than hurt Harry, he merely casts a spell that hurls him to the ground before making his escape.

These are hardly the actions of a cold-hearted murderer and a loyal Death Eater. The irony is that in killing Dumbledore, Snape has proved once and for all that he is on Dumbledore's side.

So there you have it in black and white: Snape is good. He's horrible, but you can't get away from the fact that he's on Harry's side. But the million dollar question remains: What is Snape going to do in Book 7?

Snape's Future

Admittedly, the future doesn't look too rosy for Snape. He is an outcast from civilized society, on the run for a killing he committed to help the cause of good, and is trusted only by his enemies. The Death Eaters now believe in him and respect him as never before, but he still can't afford to drop his guard for a moment in case he gives himself away. And there is virtually nothing he can do to make his genuine allies believe that he is still loyal.

Virtually nothing, but not actually nothing. There is, in fact, one thing that he can do to convince them. He can sacrifice himself for the cause.

Throughout Book 7, Snape will continue to pose as a loyal Death Eater. He will be Voldemort's right-hand man, trusted and honored beyond any other, always given the ear and the favor of the Dark Lord. He will be at Voldemort's side throughout his campaign to kill Harry now that Dumbledore is out of the way. He will have in his hands all of the information he could ever have wanted about Voldemort—information that could easily be used to defeat the Dark Lord once and for all. But now, when he finally knows everything, the Order will no longer trust him.

Yet Snape will still have a vital part to play in Voldemort's downfall. Just when Voldemort thinks he is about to win, his trusted servant will turn against him. Snape will be prepared to sacrifice himself to bring down the Dark Lord. And in laying his life on the line, he will have done the only possible thing that could have convinced Harry and the remaining members of the Order that he never betrayed them after all.

But there's an even more ironic twist in the tale. When Voldemort first tried to kill Harry, he was faced by Lily, who was willing to die in Harry's place, and in dying gave Harry the protection that saved him from the curse that should have ended his life. Now, seventeen years later, the Dark Lord will once again be in a position to take Harry's life. Harry will no longer be under his mother's protection because it was removed when Voldemort was regenerated with his blood [GOF, p. 642]. But unexpectedly, unbelievably, Voldemort will once again find someone standing between himself and his quarry, someone else willing to die for the cause. This time it will be Snape, finally paying off the life debt in his mind that he owes to James and Harry, and avenging the death of Lily, the girl he loved.

In this final battle, Snape will drop his mask of Occlumency for the first time in eighteen years and Voldemort will finally see what is really in Snape's mind, a catalogue of his treachery against the Dark Lord.

Voldemort's rage will be fierce, but he will be forced into a stalemate. If Voldemort wants Harry, then he will have to defeat Snape, but if he kills Snape he will bestow on Harry exactly the same protection that he got from Lily all those years ago. Voldemort will realize from his previous error with Lily that he doesn't need to kill Snape to get at Harry; he just needs to get him out of the way. And so a duel between the two most powerful wizards left in the world will begin, and it is highly likely that if Snape is unable to defeat Voldemort directly, he will cast a spell to sacrifice them both. After all, Snape has already proven his intense loyalty to the Order's cause by killing Dumbledore and making himself an outcast. He is no coward and will be willing to make this ultimate sacrifice.

So will Snape make it out alive in the end? Since the publication of HBP, many have assumed that his number would be up at the end of the series, and that he would sacrifice himself to defeat the Dark Lord. However, in July 2006, J.K.R. gave an interview in which she stated that someone who was originally going to die at the end had been reprieved:

> **J.K.R.:** *The final chapter is hidden away, although it has now changed very slightly. One character got a reprieve, but I have to say two die that I didn't intend to die.* [Richard and Judy interview, 2006]

Could the character who is saved be Severus Snape?

A lot of people are theorizing that Snape will be a goner after Book 7, but these people are forgetting one crucial thing: the life debt. Snape has saved Harry's life on many occasions and Harry is now in serious life debt to Snape. He will have to do everything in his power to save Snape. And if Harry succeeds, Snape will once more feel indebted to a Potter, and it will make him very unhappy indeed.

Voldemort's Horcruxes: Questions, Questions

The existence of Voldemort's Horcruxes is one of the biggest revelations to come out of HBP. Finally, we know the answer to one of the most puzzling mysteries of the series: why Voldemort did not die the night he first tried to kill young Harry Potter. But in answering this question, the Horcrux revelation posed hundreds of new questions. What are Horcruxes? How are they made? What is their purpose? How many Horcruxes does Voldemort have?

Some of these questions are answered directly in HBP, while others are left open for debate. The most vital questions, however, have only partial answers. To answer these questions, we need to gather information not just from the latest book in the series, but from the series as a whole. The most important Horcrux questions, then, are as follows: What specific objects did Voldemort choose to use as Horcruxes? Where are Voldemort's Horcruxes located? What is the significance of each choice?

Let's start with what little is known about Horcruxes in general. According to Horace Slughorn, "A Horcrux is the word used for an object in which a person has concealed part of their soul" [HBP, p. 497]. To make a Horcrux, a person must split his or her soul in two. This can only be done by murdering another human being: "Killing rips the soul apart. The wizard intent upon creating a Horcrux would use the damage to his advantage" [HBP, p. 498]. In other words, someone who wanted to make a Horcrux would first commit murder, splitting his or her soul, and then enclose the torn fragment of soul within an object, using a Dark spell.

Why Did Voldemort Make the Horcruxes?

What was Voldemort's purpose in creating the Horcruxes? The answer is simple: Horcruxes render the person who makes them immortal:

> *"Well, you split your soul, you see," said Slughorn, "and hide part of it in an object outside the body. Then, even if one's body is attacked or destroyed, one cannot die, for part of the soul remains earthbound and undamaged."* [HBP, p. 497]

Tom Riddle learned what Horcruxes were at age sixteen, and he probably made his first Horcrux around that time. It was at age fifteen that Tom murdered his father and his paternal grandparents, so he had already completed the first step in the creation of a Horcrux. As Lord Voldemort, Tom would go on to commit many more murders, splitting his soul over and again and concealing the fragments in Horcruxes. It was the existence of these Horcruxes that saved him later, when he was struck by his own Killing Curse as it rebounded off Harry Potter. Despite being hit with the curse, Voldemort was not killed. He was reduced to little more than essence and vapor, but he did not die. Eventually, Voldemort was able to resurrect himself, returning to both body and power. This act would not have been possible but for the existence of his Horcruxes.

How Many Horcruxes Are There?

If Voldemort remains immortal for as long as his Horcruxes exist, wouldn't it make sense for him to make as many Horcruxes as possible? After all, splitting his soul in two would give Voldemort some power to cheat death, but it would leave him with only one backup should anything happen to the first. For someone as obsessed with the idea of eternal life as Voldemort, having only one backup wouldn't have been good enough:

> "...would one Horcrux be much use? Can you only split your soul once? Wouldn't it be better, make you stronger, to have your soul in more pieces...?" [HBP, p. 498]

Dumbledore assumed that Voldemort split his soul not into two pieces, but into seven fragments. It seems that Dumbledore was right. First of all, seven is a powerfully magical number. Even as a young man, Voldemort was obsessed with ideas of power. He may have thought that choosing a significant magical number, like seven, would give his Horcruxes added power. When discussing Horcruxes with Slughorn as a student, Voldemort asks the rhetorical question, "Isn't seven the most powerfully magical number...?" [HBP, p. 498].

In addition to power, Voldemort is also obsessed with legacy and pride. He wants to be remembered forever. In HBP, Dumbledore states that Voldemort has always had a "determination to carve for himself a startling place in magical history" [HBP, p. 504]. By using obvious magical symbols like the number seven, Voldemort would only add to his aura and cement his legend in history.

Even at sixteen, Voldemort planned to commit what Slughorn describes as "the supreme act of evil" [HBP, p. 498]—murdering enough people to split his soul seven times. Doing so would ensure not only that Voldemort could not be directly killed, but also that his soul would be divided by the most powerful of all magical numbers.

Dumbledore also notes that the carelessness with which Voldemort treated one particular Horcrux is further proof that he had a number of them—so many that the loss of one would hardly matter:

> *"...he was being remarkably blasé about that precious fragment of his soul concealed within it....The careless way in which Voldemort regarded this Horcrux....suggested that he must have made—or been planning to make—more Horcruxes, so that the loss of his first would not be so detrimental."* [HBP, p. 501]

Indeed, Voldemort did create more than one Horcrux. In splitting his soul seven times, he intended to create six of them [HBP, pp. 500-503]. Of these six Horcruxes, two have been destroyed (the diary and the ring), one is missing (the locket stolen by R.A.B. that even Voldemort doesn't know about), and three remain unaccounted for. This means that for Harry to finish the task he and Dumbledore started, he has to locate and destroy at least four more Horcruxes before he can go after Voldemort. Of these four, only two are known objects. The other two are unknown objects, although evidence in the books suggests what they are likely to be.

What Are the Horcruxes?

Readers get their first glimpse of one of Voldemort's Horcruxes in *Chamber of Secrets*. It is Tom Riddle's diary—"a small, thin book" with a "shabby black cover" [COS, p. 230]. The diary is nondescript but it proves to be a highly magical, extraordinarily sinister object. The diary Horcrux acts as a conduit; it allows young Ginny Weasley to pour her emotions into its pages, and it in turn pours a bit of Voldemort's soul back into her. Ginny's emotional relationship with the diary enables the piece of Voldemort's soul enclosed within the diary to possess her, eventually draining enough of her life force to leave the diary's pages. Although Voldemort had intended his Horcruxes to be used as safeguards against death, the diary Horcrux had a second purpose. As Dumbledore says:

> "...that diary had been intended as a weapon....it worked as
> a Horcrux is supposed to work.... But there could be no doubt
> that Riddle really wanted that diary read, wanted the piece of
> his soul to inhabit or possess somebody else..." [HBP, pp. 500-501]

There is nothing to suggest that the remaining Horcruxes are also intended to be used as weapons, but that doesn't make them harmless. Indeed, in destroying another of Voldemort's Horcruxes, Dumbledore is severely injured, and he carries the scars for the rest of his life.

The diary is the only Horcrux made out of an object that was not hidden or protected in any way. It was made quite accessible—we explain why below—and this is what leads to its destruction. Harry obtains and destroys it at the end of his second year at Hogwarts. Unlike the diary (and except for any Horcruxes that are living beings and not objects), the rest of Voldemort's Horcruxes not only have been hidden, but have also been protected with a variety of spells, creatures, and only Voldemort knows what else to keep them safe.

The second Horcrux to be found and destroyed is the one that cost Dumbledore the use of his arm. This Horcrux was originally Salazar Slytherin's gold ring. This ring, with the Peverell coat of arms engraved on its large black stone, was one of Voldemort's family heirlooms. It had been in the Gaunt family for centuries, the Gaunts being Slytherin's last living descendents and Voldemort being the last of the Gaunt line [HBP, pp. 207-208]. Voldemort took the ring from his uncle, Morfin Gaunt, after framing Morfin for the murder of Voldemort's own father and paternal grandparents. Voldemort then wore Slytherin's ring for a short while during his time at Hogwarts (he is wearing it in one of the memories Harry views in the Pensieve [HBP, p. 369]), but he stopped wearing it once he "succeeded in sealing a piece of his soul inside it" [HBP, p. 504]. We don't know if he hid the ring immediately after making it into a Horcrux, but we do know that this particular Horcrux was found and successfully destroyed. The remaining Horcruxes are still intact.

The black-stoned ring was not the only possession of Slytherin's that Voldemort decided to turn into a Horcrux. Early in his career with Borgin and Burkes, Voldemort visited a rich, elderly witch named Hepzibah Smith. Hepzibah was distantly descended from Helga Hufflepuff, and she had in her possession a "small golden cup with two finely wrought handles" [HBP, p. 436] that had once belonged to Hufflepuff. In addition to Hufflepuff's cup, Hepzibah had something of far greater value to Voldemort, an object he wanted so badly he was willing to kill for it. Hepzibah had a heavy gold locket with "an ornate, serpentine *S*" [HBP, p. 437]. It was Slytherin's locket, the same one that had once belonged to Voldemort's mother [HBP, p. 437]. After seeing these items, Voldemort killed Hepzibah, framed her house elf for the crime, and stole both Slytherin's locket and Hufflepuff's cup before disappearing himself. There is little doubt that the cup and the locket later became Horcruxes numbers three and four.

Although Voldemort was especially fascinated with Slytherin (due to his desire to cement his legend in magical history), he wanted an object that had belonged to each of the four Hogwarts founders to turn into a Horcrux. He had something from both Slytherin and Hufflepuff. That left only Rowena Ravenclaw and Godric Gryffindor.

We don't know whether or not Voldemort was able to locate something of Ravenclaw's, but it is doubtful that he found anything of Gryffindor's. The only known relics of Godric Gryffindor are the ruby-encrusted sword Harry pulled from the Sorting Hat, and the Sorting Hat itself. Both of these objects are kept in the Headmaster's office, and Voldemort did not have access to either of them. Even though he was briefly in Dumbledore's office when interviewing for the D.A.D.A. position [HBP, pp. 441-46], he had neither the time nor the opportunity to work any complicated Dark spells. He certainly did not create a Horcrux right under the nose of Albus Dumbledore, the most powerful wizard in the world and the only wizard Voldemort is said to have feared. That is why, like Dumbledore, we are "forced to conclude that he never fulfilled his ambition of collecting four founders' objects. He definitely had two—he may have found three" [HBP, p. 506], but Gryffindor's relics were locked safely in Dumbledore's office, out of Voldemort's reach. Because it seems certain that Voldemort was unable to find anything belonging to Gryffindor, the fifth Horcrux is probably something belonging to Ravenclaw. What this object is, however, is anyone's guess.

The sixth Horcrux, the final Horcrux Voldemort intended to make, is his most peculiar choice of all. Dumbledore believed that the sixth Horcrux was not an object, but rather Voldemort's faithful snake, Nagini. It is inadvisable to turn a living creature into a Horcrux because the creature can act independently, possibly endangering both itself and the piece of soul it carries [HBP, p. 506]. However, Voldemort was seemingly at a loss for other options when he sealed a piece of his soul inside his faithful pet. According to Dumbledore, Voldemort "reserved the process of making Horcruxes for particularly significant deaths" [HBP, p. 506]. He still had one Horcrux left to make the evening he went to Godric's Hollow in search of young Harry Potter. The death Voldemort had in mind was Harry's, but his plan was thwarted and Voldemort was torn from his body before he could kill Harry and create his final Horcrux. Reduced to a formless vapor for thirteen years, Voldemort could not even raise a wand, never mind create a Horcrux. Therefore, when he was returned to his body and power, Voldemort was anxious to create a sixth Horcrux, to split his soul into the seven pieces he had originally intended. Having already been defeated once, Voldemort did not want to wait any longer than necessary to create his last Horcrux. Therefore, when Voldemort killed an old Muggle man who had once worked for his father, he used that opportunity to make what he believed to be his sixth Horcrux.

Why choose Nagini? Nagini is Voldemort's faithful pet. She helped him return to a physical form by giving him some of her venom. Voldemort used a potion "concocted from unicorn blood, and the snake venom Nagini provided" to fashion himself a weak, rudimentary body that he could use until he could be restored to his own form [GOF, p. 656]. Nagini then continued to sustain Voldemort in some way until he was able to return to his former body. We know this because Voldemort once chastised Wormtail, saying that he "need[ed] feeding every few hours" and if Wormtail were to leave there would be no one "to milk Nagini" [GOF, p. 9]. From this, it seems evident that Voldemort depended on his faithful snake for his physical well-being for some time. Nagini was also present in the graveyard the night he was restored to his former body and power [GOF, p. 639]. Nagini is much closer to Voldemort than any of his followers. He has been known to possess her and have her do his bidding [OOTP, pp. 532-33]. They communicate with one another in Parseltongue and "she underlines the Slytherin connection, which enhances Lord Voldemort's mystique" [HBP, p. 506]. In short, Voldemort has a strong affiliation with the snake. As Dumbledore says in regards to Voldemort and Nagini, "he is perhaps as fond of her as he can be of anything" [HBP, p. 506]. Although Nagini is a living creature, it makes sense that Voldemort chose her as his sixth Horcrux because he prizes her so greatly.

Where Are the Horcruxes?

Knowing what to look for is only half of the problem in searching for Horcruxes; the other half is knowing where to look. Not only did Voldemort choose objects of significance to transform into Horcruxes, he chose places of significance in which to hide them. Since not much is known about Voldemort's early life, and even less about the first few years after he left Hogwarts, locating these places of significance is difficult at best.

For special reasons, the diary Horcrux was not hidden. Voldemort placed the diary under the care of his faithful servant, Lucius Malfoy. Voldemort instructed Lucius to pass the diary to an unsuspecting person who could then be used to reopen the Chamber of Secrets. Unfortunately, he did not tell Lucius what the diary really was, and Lucius was careless with this piece of Voldemort's soul. Although Voldemort wanted Lucius to smuggle the diary into Hogwarts, "Lucius was supposed to wait for Voldemort's say-so, and he never received it, for Voldemort vanished shortly after giving him the diary" [HBP, p. 508]. So Lucius was working of his own volition when he slipped the diary to Ginny Weasley. Although Harry physically destroyed the diary Horcrux, Lucius was the one who placed it in harm's way by not waiting for his master's orders before passing the book along. Voldemort would likely not trust any of the remaining Horcruxes to his followers after the loss of the diary, so we can assume that the other Horcruxes are better hidden than the diary was, and that they are protected in some way.

The ring Horcrux was well concealed. Voldemort hid it "in the shack where his ancestors had once lived" [HBP, p. 504]. This location was of importance to Voldemort because it was where he first came into contact with the ring, and where the last of his magical relatives had lived. The ring stayed hidden in the remains of the Gaunt cottage until Dumbledore visited the ruins. Noticing signs of magical concealment, Dumbledore was able to find the ring and destroy the piece of soul it contained. The ring was last seen lying idly on one of the spindle-legged tables in Dumbledore's office, the large, black stone cracked through [HBP, p. 215].

The locket Horcrux is the last Horcrux to have been located (although its current location is a bit of a mystery). It has a much more interesting history than either the diary or the ring. Voldemort originally hid the locket Horcrux in a cave—the same cave he had used to terrify two other children when he was a boy [HBP, p. 547]. Although Voldemort protected this Horcrux with a number of enchantments and horrifying creatures, the locket did not remain in the cave for long.

Harry and Dumbledore visit this cave in search of the Horcrux. While they do retrieve a locket from inside the cave, it turns out not to be Slytherin's locket at all. What Harry and Dumbledore take from the cave is a decoy left in place of the actual Horcrux, which had been removed several years before by the enigmatic R.A.B. [HBP, p. 609].

Like Dumbledore and Harry, R.A.B. had discovered that Voldemort was making and hiding Horcruxes. In an attempt to hurt Voldemort (though R.A.B. seems to have known that he could not stop him), R.A.B. took the Horcrux and left behind the fake locket and a note, which expressed his desire to destroy the Horcrux and his hope that Voldemort would one day be defeated [HBP, p. 609].

While R.A.B. had every intention of destroying the locket, it is possible that he died before he got the chance to do so. So where is the locket now?

That depends on the identity of R.A.B. If you believe, as we do, that R.A.B is—or rather was—Regulus Black, then you know exactly where R.A.B. took it after leaving the cave. While cleaning out Number 12, Grimmauld Place, the former home of Regulus Black, Harry and the Weasleys come across "a heavy locket that none of them could open" [OOTP, p. 116]. This locket is only mentioned in passing, but it seems ominously significant now. We believe this locket is the locket Horcrux that Regulus stole from the cave.

The locket Horcrux was last seen in Grimmauld Place, but that doesn't mean it is still there. Mundungus Fletcher has been stealing things from Grimmauld Place to sell on the black market [HBP, pp. 245-47]. It is possible that Mundungus has stolen the locket and sold it, not realizing what it was (for more evidence on this subject, please see the chapter on the identity of R.A.B.). It is also possible, however, that the locket was hidden before Mundungus had the chance to steal it. Kreacher, the Black family house elf, smuggled many objects off to his sleeping quarters to save them from being thrown away when the Order adopted Grimmauld Place as its head-quarters [OOTP, pp. 109-10]. In fact, Kreacher is seen sidling into the room right after the locket is discovered at Grimmauld Place. Sirius confronts him, saying, "Every time you show up pretending to be cleaning, you sneak something off to your room so we can't throw it out" [OOTP, pp. 109-10]. Indeed, Kreacher's room does contain an assortment of Black family heirlooms that he managed to save from the garbage bin [OOTP, p. 504]. It is possible, then, that Kreacher was able to steal the locket without anyone noticing and hide it in his quarters. If this is the case, the locket remains at Grimmauld Place with all the other Dark Artifacts Kreacher has stashed away. It is equally possible, and perhaps more probable, however, that the locket was pawned by Mundungus.

Where are the remaining Horcruxes hidden? The sixth Horcrux, Nagini, is not hidden at all. Voldemort seems to like having her by his side. As for Hufflepuff's cup and the object that had been Raven-claw's, we can only guess. Wherever they are hidden, it will be in a place that holds meaning for Voldemort. He may have returned to the Muggle orphanage where he was raised to hide something, since it was at the orphanage that he first learned the truth about his magical powers. But since the orphanage is a Muggle building, it seems doubtful. A likelier place for him to have hidden some-thing is Hogwarts:

> *"…Voldemort was…more attached to this school than he has ever been to a person. Hogwarts was where he had been happiest; the first and only place he had felt at home."* [HBP, p. 431]

Voldemort had made at least one Horcrux—possibly more—before he graduated from Hogwarts. He may have had the time, as a student, to hide one of his Horcruxes on the Hogwarts grounds. He may even have hidden one in the castle itself. But with Dumbledore in the school, Voldemort had to remain on his best behavior so as not to call attention to himself after framing Hagrid for opening the Chamber of Secrets. It is unlikely he would have risked hiding a Horcrux right under Dumbledore's nose, but we will just have to wait for the last book to know for sure.

What Is the Significance of Each Choice?

Why did Voldemort choose those particular objects when he decided to make Horcruxes? Why not pick items at random and hide them in even more random locations so that they might never be found? That is what Harry wonders, but Dumbledore tells him:

> *"…Lord Voldemort liked to collect trophies, and he preferred objects with a powerful magical history. His pride…his determination to carve for himself a startling place in magical history; these things suggest to me that Voldemort would have chosen his Horcruxes with some care, favoring objects worthy of the honor."* [HBP, p. 504]

The first Horcrux was the diary. The diary was an old, battered book from a shop in Muggle London. While it was not much to look at, it contained information that was of extreme importance to Voldemort: "The diary…was proof that he was the Heir of Slytherin" [HBP, pp. 504-505]. Voldemort is proud, and he wanted people to know this about him. He thought the knowledge that he was descended from Slytherin would somehow make up for the fact that his father was a Muggle—a fact he was so ashamed of that he changed his name from Tom Riddle to Lord Voldemort. The diary recorded the facts that Voldemort could both open the Chamber of Secrets and control Slytherin's monster, highlighting Voldemort's proud ties to Slytherin [HBP, pp. 500-501; COS, p. 312].

Voldemort placed his precious diary in the hands of Lucius Malfoy, a man he considered one of his most faithful servants. By choosing to hide the diary with Lucius, it was made evident that Lucius's allegiance belonged to Voldemort, even though Lucius was still in with the Ministry at the time [GOF, p. 650]. This act illustrated the power Voldemort was able to wield over other witches and wizards. As we all know, Voldemort is all about displays of power. Both the diary and its placement with Lucius were of significance to Voldemort. They were chosen because they demonstrated his Slytherin lineage and the great authority he held over others.

The second Horcrux was Slytherin's ring. This ring was important because it had once belonged to Slytherin and had been in Voldemort's family for generations. In hiding the ring, Voldemort returned it to the very place from which he had taken it. Crazed and downtrodden as the Gaunts were, they were pure-bloods and the last descendents of Slytherin. These were two facts that Voldemort prized, embracing the pure-blood part of his heritage while denying, and ultimately destroying, everything (his father, his grandparents, and his name) that associated him with the Muggle part of his heritage. Again, both object and location were significant to Voldemort.

The locket Horcrux was important for the same reasons as the ring. Like the ring, the locket had once belonged to Slytherin. The locket bore Slytherin's mark, had magical powers, and had been owned by Voldemort's mother before he was born. Committing murder to retrieve this item, Voldemort made the locket into a

Horcrux and hid it in a place of importance to himself, the cave where he used his magical abilities as a child to intimidate other children and exert power over them. The locket, apart from any magic that it possessed, was a symbol of Slytherin, and as such it commanded a certain level of respect. The cave was a place where Voldemort was also able to command a level of respect, though the other children regarded him with fear rather than admiration.

Hufflepuff's cup is significant to Voldemort because it had once belonged to one of the four Hogwarts founders. As Dumbledore tells Harry, "Four objects from the four founders would, I am sure, have exerted a powerful pull over Voldemort's imagination" [HBP, p. 505].

Why so? Because the Hogwarts founders were powerfully magical, and their possessions are valuable on a number of levels. Not only are they priceless artifacts, they are a piece of magical history. Prideful and ambitious, Voldemort wanted to carve out his own place in wizarding history, just as the founders had done in their time, and he was willing to go to any lengths to do so. Perhaps Voldemort felt that using the possessions of powerful witches and wizards as his Horcruxes would lend him some additional power. Voldemort wanted to split his soul seven times because seven is the most powerful of magical numbers. If he was willing to go to that length because of the magic attributed to a number, surely he would choose objects of great magical significance as his Horcruxes. Any former possession of the Hogwarts founders is a cultural artifact in the magical community. It was in Voldemort's nature to want to hoard these precious objects, personalizing them by turning them into Horcruxes, and thereby associating his name with the names of the four founders.

Voldemort would also want artifacts from Hogwarts because, as we mentioned, Hogwarts was "the first and only place he had felt at home" [HBP p. 431]. Furthermore, Hogwarts "is a stronghold of ancient magic," and the cup itself was said to possess certain magical powers. We all know that lust for power is always Voldemort's most compelling instinct [HBP, pp. 431 & 436]. Hufflepuff's cup represented magic and power to Voldemort, which was why he wanted it for one of his Horcruxes. We don't yet know where this cup is hidden, but there is little doubt that the cup is a Horcrux, or that Voldemort values it highly.

The fifth object, if it truly was something of Ravenclaw's, is important for the same reasons as Slytherin's ring, Slytherin's locket, and Hufflepuff's cup. Voldemort wanted an object from each of the Hogwarts founders. We have yet to see any items belonging to Ravenclaw in the books, but if the other founders' item can be taken as examples, it is likely to be a small, personal object. Additionally, it will probably bear some symbol marking it as Ravenclaw's. Slytherin's locket bears his mark, Slytherin's ring has the Peverell coat of arms on it, Hufflepuff's cup has a small engraving of a badger on the side, and Gryffindor's sword has a ruby-encrusted handle. Whatever small, personal object of Ravenclaw's Voldemort may have been able to find, it will likely illustrate its connection to Ravenclaw in some way.

The sixth Horcrux, Nagini, is important to Voldemort for several reasons:

> "...She underlines the Slytherin connection, which enhances Lord Voldemort's mystique...he is perhaps as fond of her as he can be of anything; he certainly likes to keep her close, and he seems to have an unusual amount of control over her, even for a Parselmouth." [HBP, pp. 506-507]

If we assume, as Dumbledore did, that Nagini is the sixth Horcrux, it becomes clear exactly how fond Voldemort is of this creature. It cannot be said that Voldemort is actually close to anyone, not even his most faithful servants, and yet he seems to care a great deal for this snake. Voldemort has delved so far into the Dark Arts that he does not have many human characteristics left. Even his appearance is inhuman and snakelike: "The thin man stepped out of the cauldron…[he had] wide, livid scarlet eyes and a nose that was flat as a snake's with slits for nostrils" [GOF, p. 643]. Voldemort has spent so much time possessing Nagini and communicating with her in Parseltongue that he may well have developed an unnatural fondness for her. Perhaps he identifies with her on some level. Nagini is a constant presence in Voldemort's life, always by his side and ready to do his bidding. Not human, Nagini lacks the selfish desires that characterize the Death Eaters. She is able to protect herself, and since she is almost always with Voldemort, it would be difficult for anyone to steal her or kill her. All of these are good reasons why Voldemort might choose to make Nagini the sixth Horcrux.

Is There a Seventh Horcrux?

We know that Voldemort intended to split his soul into seven pieces, making six Horcruxes. However, even the best of intentions sometimes run astray. Is it possible that Voldemort created a seventh, accidental Horcrux? A Horcrux even he isn't aware of? We believe so. What, then, is this unintentional Horcrux? We believe the accidental Horcrux is none other than Harry Potter.

This is another argument that has separated Harry Potter fans and caused many debates; it even has its own chapter in this book. For both sides of the argument, check out "Chapter 12: Is Harry a Horcrux?" The basic overview, however, is that Voldemort intended to make a Horcrux the night he meant to kill Harry Potter. Voldemort had made all of the necessary preparations when the unthinkable happened—his Avada Kedavra backfired. A great deal of magic was released that night: ripping Voldemort from his body, destroying the Potters' home, and leaving Harry with his infamous lightening-bolt scar. With all the unintentional magic flying around Godric's Hollow that night, the Horcrux spell Voldemort had prepared was also released. That's our argument, at least. For a look at the evidence we have to back up this argument, flip the page to that chapter now.

Is Harry a Horcrux?

The thorny topic of Harry being a Horcrux has caused much debate among readers. Is he a Horcrux or not?

Harry Is a Horcrux

One thing that nobody disputes is the fact that there is a magical link between Voldemort and Harry. The focal point of that link is Harry's scar. The exact nature of the connection isn't fully understood (not by us readers, anyway), but we do know that it works on a number of levels. Each one has a window into the mind of the other. Harry frequently senses Voldemort's emotions and even sees through his eyes on occasion [GOF, pp. 576-77]. Voldemort himself, as the more powerful wizard, has learned to control the link from his side so that he can plant images in Harry's brain at will [OOTP, pp. 726-

28]. Later he employs Occlumency in order to block the connection altogether when he realizes that it works both ways [HBP, p. 59].

Harry also shares a number of Voldemort's skills, such as the gift of Parseltongue, the ability to speak to snakes [COS, p. 195]. They looked a lot alike before the Dark Lord's appearance changed beyond recognition, as Tom Riddle himself points out.

> *"There are strange likenesses between us, after all. Even you*
> *must have noticed. Both half-bloods, orphans, raised by*
> *Muggles. Probably the only two Parselmouths to come to*
> *Hogwarts since the great Slytherin himself. We even* look
> *something alike...."* [COS, p. 317]

They were also selected by brother wands [SS, p. 85].

What we don't know is exactly why all these things are true. There are many possible explanations, but no cold, hard facts. The close bond between the two enemies, however, does highly suggest that Harry is a Horcrux.

Godric's Hollow

Harry's scar is, we are told, a relic of Voldemort's attempt to kill him [SS, p. 55]. The spell Voldemort chose was Avada Kedavra. But Avada Kedavra famously leaves no mark whatsoever on the victim's body [GOF, p. 216]. Yes, the curse was blocked, but why would that produce a scar? There's no evidence of blocked curses causing scars anywhere else in the book. In fact, Snape blocks an awful lot of curses from Harry after killing Dumbledore [HBP, pp. 602-603], but Snape doesn't erupt with open wounds. What does this mean? It means that Harry's scar is not a result of the Avada Kedavra curse, or of the fact that it was blocked. It must be the result of something else.

Let's go back to the mysterious connection between Harry and Voldemort. Those who argue that Harry isn't a Horcrux put this connection down to a transfer of powers caused by the blocked curse. But, again, there is no evidence anywhere in the books that a blocked curse can produce this effect. If it could, there should now be so many windows between Snape's mind and Harry's mind that you could hardly count them, and Harry should be the spitting image of Snape. But blocking a curse doesn't forge a link of any kind. The link, and the scar, are both due to something else.

The truth is that murdering the Potters probably wasn't the only thing on Voldemort's mind when he went to Godric's Hollow on that evening back when Harry was only a year old. Yes, he was going to kill Harry, but he was also planning to do something else. As Dumbledore himself tells Harry, "I am sure that he was intending to make his final Horcrux with your death" [HBP, p. 506]. This would've given Voldemort the seven-part soul that he believed would guarantee him immortality.

Voldemort liked to reserve his creation of Horcruxes for significant murders. And what could be more significant than murdering Harry, his enemy from the prophecy? But things didn't quite go according to plan.

It Was an Accident

Voldemort may have taken with him the object he intended to turn into his last Horcrux on the night of October 31. What it was we will probably never know, but it is reasonable to assume that in addition to having the object itself, some preparation is required to create a Horcrux. J.K.R. has been very vague about the nature of the magic required; the only information we have comes in a single sentence from Horace Slughorn:

> *"There is a spell, do not ask me, I don't know!" said Slughorn,*
> *shaking his head like an old elephant bothered by mosquitoes.*
> [HBP, p. 498]

The lack of clear information is deliberate, designed to make it impossible to rule out the sequence of events described here. We simply don't know if the spell has to be cast in advance of the killing, at the same time as the killing, or after the killing. But if the spell was cast before or while Voldemort was trying to kill Harry, it is entirely possible that Harry was accidentally made into a Horcrux, even though the Killing Curse was repelled.

What happened at the Potters' house when the Avada Kedavra was cast, with curses flying all over the place, was mayhem, and a lot happened that can't be put down to a simple Killing Curse. A scar was burned into Harry's forehead, of course. But rather more eye-catching was the fact that the entire house was destroyed—peculiar when we know that Avada Kedavra does no damage to the surrounding area [HBP, p. 366].

So there must have been a lot of very powerful uncontrolled magic whizzing around that night. In the midst of the rebounding Killing Curse, and whatever it was that destroyed the house, the Horcrux spell that Voldemort had prepared could've fired accidentally. He had already committed murder—two murders, in fact (those of James and Lily)—so his soul was already split, ready to enter whatever object it was directed into. But because of the magical mayhem that ensues following Voldemort's Killing Curse, the new piece of his soul was almost certainly not directed into the object that he had chosen. It could've entered Harry instead. The scar would be evidence of that, and the window into Voldemort's mind and the transfer of powers are the possible results of it.

In HBP, when Harry asks Dumbledore whether Voldemort can feel when his Horcruxes are destroyed, Dumbledore says no [HBP, p. 507]. If Voldemort cannot feel a Horcrux being destroyed, he probably can't feel one being created, either. That would explain why Voldemort would be unaware of Harry's status as a Horcrux.

Dumbledore Knew

Voldemort, brilliant though he is, can be prone to the odd astonishing lapse of memory. He forgets that phoenix tears have healing properties [COS, p. 322]. He forgets that sacrificing your life for someone gives that person magical protection against your killer [COS, p. 322]. He has also been totally surprised by the Priori Incantatem effect [GOF, p. 663]. This probably explains why he didn't realize the significance of Harry's scar for such a long time. Dumbledore, on the other hand, realized right away. He knew that Avada Kedavra leaves no mark, and he suspected what Harry was right from the start.

But Dumbledore likes to protect people. Just as he resolves to protect Harry from the knowledge of his true destiny by concealing the prophecy from him until he turns fifteen [OOTP, pp. 825-26], so he decides to protect Harry from the idea that he is probably carrying around a piece of Voldemort's soul inside him. Nevertheless, he sometimes deliberately and sometimes accidentally leaves a trail of clues for Harry to follow. The first and most obvious is his suggestion that Nagini may be a Horcrux [HBP, p. 506]. In saying this, he gives Harry (and us) an anvil-sized clue. Animals (and people are animals, too) can be Horcruxes. If Nagini can be a Horcrux, so can Harry.

Dumbledore drops another clue that refers to Nagini when he says that he is suspicious about the level of control that Voldemort has over her: "… he certainly likes to keep her close, and he seems to have an unusual amount of control over her, even for a Parselmouth" [HBP, p. 507]. Dumbledore is referring to exactly the same kind of window-in-the-mind effect that Voldemort shares with Harry. Voldemort cannot control Harry's actions, but he can place images in his mind whenever he wants to. Nagini is only a snake, and Voldemort is a Parselmouth, so he can use the window to virtually control her, even when he is not possessing her.

Dumbledore presents other little clues as well. When Harry is devastated by the death of Sirius, Dumbledore says something rather odd: "Harry, suffering like this proves you are still a man!" [OOTP, p. 824]. Just what does Dumbledore mean by "still a man"? For him to use this phrase is certainly a slip of the tongue, coming as it does at an emotionally charged time. It is a direct reference to the belief that Harry is carrying something less than human inside him.

On another occasion, Dumbledore produces a snake made of smoke from an instrument in his office and asks it whether it is "in essence divided" [OOTP, p. 470]. This episode occurs right after Harry sees through Voldemort's eyes as Voldemort is possessing Nagini [OOTP, p. 468]—which makes it clear why Dumbledore is asking the question. Dumbledore is referring to the link between Harry's soul and that of the Dark Lord.

Dumbledore realizes, of course, that the news that you might be one of Voldemort's Horcruxes is hard to bear, so he decides to wait until he thinks Harry is ready to hear it. Now that Dumbledore is dead, it seems he may have waited too long.

Voldemort Knows

Those who argue that Harry isn't a Horcrux usually base their argument on the fact that Voldemort has tried to kill Harry on numerous occasions—and Voldemort would never try to destroy his own Horcrux. Therefore, either Harry isn't a Horcrux or, if he is, Voldemort doesn't know. Voldemort *didn't* know it until relatively recently. But he knows it now.

Voldemort has missed a lot of clues along the way: Harry's scar, the fact that Harry can open the Chamber of Secrets even though he isn't the Heir of Slytherin, the physical likeness. But then something happens that finally fills him in. Right at the end of the battle at the Department of Mysteries, Voldemort possesses Harry [OOTP, p. 816]. He is driven out pretty quickly when Harry remembers Sirius and his mind is flooded with love, the emotion that Voldemort hates and fears so much. However, he is in there long enough to realize if part of his soul was already residing within Harry. Voldemort will have figured out that, way back when he attacked the Potters, he accidentally turned Harry into one of his Horcruxes.

His immediate change in policy suggests this knowledge. For sixteen years, Voldemort has been singlemindedly driven by his desire to kill Harry Potter, but suddenly, he decides to leave Harry alone and go after Dumbledore instead? That makes zero sense if Harry isn't a Horcrux. But if Harry is a Horcrux, it makes perfect sense. Why? Because Voldemort would want to remove Harry's protection (Dumbledore), but he wouldn't want to destroy his Horcrux, which he now believes lies within his enemy.

There is further evidence of this in the instructions that Voldemort issues to the Death Eaters: Harry is for Voldemort only; he is not to be touched [HBP, p. 603]. Voldemort wants Harry for himself because he needs to remove the Horcrux before Harry dies. He needs to take it out of Harry and put it into another object before he disposes of his enemy. If anyone kills Harry now, the Horcrux will be lost. And even though Voldemort doesn't know about the loss of the ring Horcrux, he knows about the diary Horcrux [HBP, p. 508], and he is not eager to lose another.

Or Is He?

Despite all this powerful evidence pointing to Harry's status as a Horcrux, Albus Dumbledore makes a puzzling statement. Having already ascertained that Slytherin's Locket, Hufflepuff's Cup, and an unspecified object belonging to Rowena Ravenclaw are likely Horcruxes [HBP, p. 505], he expresses his views on the final Horcrux as follows:

> "I think I know what the sixth Horcrux is. I wonder what you
> will say when I confess that I have been curious for a while
> about the behavior of the snake, Nagini?" [HBP, p. 506]

Dumbledore makes it clear in this conversation that he believes there are only six Horcruxes, and he names each one of them. Harry is not on his list. As J.K.R. herself has said:

> "Dumbledore's guesses are never very far wide of the mark. I
> don't want to give too much away here, but Dumbledore says,
> 'There are four out there, you've got to get rid of four, and then
> you go for Voldemort.' So that's where he is, and that's what
> he's got to do." [MuggleNet/TLC interview, 2005]

Dumbledore refers to four Horcruxes because two—the ring and the diary—have already been destroyed. He names the remaining four, and since Dumbledore is the source of all knowledge in the Harry Potter world, we should take his word for it. We must keep in mind, however, that Dumbledore isn't infallible. Other clues suggest Harry is not a Horcrux.

You Have to Mean It

Throughout the entire series, magic happens only when the spellcaster intends it to. The only exception to this is when small wizarding children produce bursts of uncontrolled magic, such as when Harry removes the glass from the boa constrictor's tank at the zoo [SS, p. 28]. These aren't specific spells, however; they are just spurts of random energy. To cast a precise spell by accident is impossible; the books show no evidence of its ever happening.

Those who suggest that Harry is a Horcrux must necessarily be convinced that he was made into one accidentally, and without Voldemort's knowledge. How else could they justify the fact the Voldemort has attempted to kill Harry (which would destroy his own Horcrux if Harry were one) on such a regular basis? In order for this to have happened, the Horcrux creation spell must have gone off by accident, and that's something that has never happened in six whole books. It is, in fact, something that simply *cannot* happen. As the students at Hogwarts are taught over and over again, the exact incantation, the exact wand movement, and the exact state of mind are all required to cast a spell: "Swish and flick, remember, swish and flick. And saying the magic words properly is very important, too" [SS, p. 171].

Two Souls in One Body

Let's look at the problem of two souls residing in one body. How could a loveless, heartless soul like Voldemort's inhabit a body—Harry's—that is full of love and compassion? As we saw in OOTP,

Voldemort cannot physically possess Harry because the love within him is too strong: "That power also saved you from possession by Voldemort, because he could not bear to reside in a body so full of the force he detests" [OOTP, p. 844].

When Voldemort *did* attempt to possess Harry, during the Ministry of Magic battle, it caused tremendous pain. Harry was in so much pain, in fact, that he genuinely wanted to die [OOTP, p. 816]. Such pain is not a normal part of the possession process—as proven when Quirrell was possessed by Voldemort in SS [ch. 17] and he seemed to feel no physical pain at all. The difference is that unlike Harry, Quirrell's soul was already corrupted when Voldemort entered his body. Quirrell admits as much:

> *"I met him when I traveled around the world. A foolish young man I was then, full of ridiculous ideas about good and evil. Lord Voldemort showed me how wrong I was. There is no good and evil, there is only power, and those too weak to seek it."*
> [SS, p. 291]

These are the words of an evil, loveless man. Harry, however, is anything but evil and loveless. And we see that for him, unlike for Quirrell, the possession process was agony because of the battle between good and evil that was happening inside his very body. But isn't being a Horcrux a type of possession? And if Harry is a Horcrux, wouldn't he have been in tremendous agony all his life?

It seems logical that Harry wouldn't have felt pain all of his life because Voldemort's powers were initially too weak to harm him until Voldemort began to regenerate himself. However, this argument forgets that Voldemort split his soul at the height of his powers, and at that moment that he split his soul, the various pieces became individual entities separate from Voldemort and his powers. These pieces would retain Voldemort's immense power whether his powers grew or shrank. We see evidence that the Horcruxes are not connected to Voldemort because Voldemort doesn't even know that R.A.B. has stolen one of them.

If Harry were a Horcrux, he should have been in constant agony because of the evil soul that lives within him. But instead, we only see Harry in pain when Voldemort tries to possess him or enter his mind. This suggests that Harry couldn't have had a part of Voldemort's soul inside him: his body would never have been able to bear it.

A Dubious Moral Message

While it's true that Dumbledore managed to remove the Horcrux from Marvolo's ring, leaving it with only a cracked stone [HBP, p. 503], removing a Horcrux from within living flesh would be quite different. The stone in Marvolo's ring was strong, but even that was damaged by the removal of the Horcrux. If Harry were to have a Horcrux removed from him, what would happen? Could human flesh really survive being subjected to the equivalent of the cracking of that stone?

The crack across the stone of the ring Horcrux constituted major damage—damage far too great for a human to sustain without being killed. Therefore, if Harry were indeed a Horcrux, and if that Horcrux is to be destroyed, Harry will die. While this possibility cannot be entirely discounted, and indeed a number of fans believe J.K.R. will choose to end the series with Harry's death, it is still extremely unlikely because of the poor moral it would impart.

J.K.R. herself has admitted that the books have a highly moral undertone:

> To what extent did you conceive Harry Potter as a moral tale?
>
> **J.K.R.:** I did not conceive it as a moral tale, the morality sprang naturally out of the story, a subtle but important difference. [World Book Day, 2004]

Wherever the morality came from, it is there, and the author has acknowledged that it is there. To have Harry killed by a Horcrux in his effort to defeat Voldemort—and indeed before he could even know whether Voldemort would be defeated—would send a dubious moral message at best. J.K.R. most likely will not do it.

There are many, many reasons why Harry will live, and we cover them throughout this book. If Harry were a Horcrux, he would probably be condemned to death, and it simply will not happen.

The Diary Horcrux

> *"Four years ago, I received what I considered certain proof that Voldemort had split his soul."* [HBP, p. 500]

This proof that Dumbledore referred to was the diary Horcrux—Voldemort's first Horcrux, made after Voldemort murdered his father and grandparents when he was still a sixteen-year-old student at Hogwarts. Voldemort turned the diary into a Horcrux during his sixth year, after persuading Horace Slughorn to tell him the little he knew about Horcruxes. We saw this meeting in the memory that Slughorn tried so desperately to conceal [HBP, p. 371]. What is especially important in this memory is what Tom Riddle was wearing at the time.

> *His right hand lay negligently upon the arm of his chair; with a jolt, Harry saw that he was wearing Marvolo's gold-and-black ring; he had already killed his father.* [HBP, p. 369]

Tom Riddle had already killed at this point, even though he knew nothing about Horcruxes. He learned what he did about Horcruxes from the first pointers Slughorn gave him during this meeting. He then presumably created his first Horcrux, the diary Horcrux, using the piece of his soul split from the earlier murder of his father. The order of these events is very important because it shows that, as long as one has committed murder, one can make a Horcrux from that murder at any time. No premeditated Horcrux spell is necessary.

This suggests that when Voldemort went to murder Harry, there was nothing he needed to set up in advance, nothing that he needed to have primed to go off, nothing that could have fired accidentally. His plan would simply have been to murder Harry, and then use the damage to his soul to create his last Horcrux in his own time. There didn't necessarily have to be a Horcrux spell already cast, so why would a savvy wizard like Voldemort have taken the risk of casting it early? He most likely wouldn't have.

Targeting Dumbledore

Assuming Harry is not a Horcrux, why does Voldemort's plan change so suddenly after OOTP? Why does he suddenly want to kill Dumbledore rather than Harry, when we all know that killing Harry has been his goal for years? Because, at the battle at the Department of Mysteries, Voldemort realized that he couldn't get at Harry without Dumbledore getting in the way.

Every time Voldemort tried to dispose of his enemy, there was Dumbledore to stop it. When he possessed Quirrell and tried to take the Sorcerer's Stone from Harry, Dumbledore arrived in the nick of time and stopped him [SS, p. 296]. When Barty Crouch Jr. (posing as Moody) was about to murder Harry, it was Dumbledore (along with Snape and McGonagall) who arrived at the door in time to stop him [GOF, p. 679]. When he was about to kill Harry at the Ministry of Magic, it was Dumbledore who deflected the Killing Curse [OOTP, p. 813].

Voldemort knows that as long as Dumbledore is alive, his chances of killing Harry are very low, which may explain why he has implemented a longer-term strategy: First Dumbledore, and then Harry. If he wants Harry, which he very badly does, he has to remove Dumbledore first.

The Transfer of Power

Although it's not clear how the transfer of power took place or why Harry got a scar, nothing proves concretely that Harry is a Horcrux. The theory that some sort of Horcrux creation spell went off accidentally—and also went wrong, so that Harry, rather than an inanimate object, became a Horcrux—is possibly little more than a wild fantasy.

It isn't important that we know why the blocked curse put some of Voldemort's powers into Harry, because nobody had ever survived Avada Kedavra before. As Barty Crouch Jr. (posing as Moody) says: "Only one known person has ever survived it, and he's sitting right in front of me" [GOF, p. 216].

When something happens that has never happened before, it will have unexpected effects. Things will happen without anyone knowing why, and that's what happened in this case. Dumbledore talked about this transfer of powers, but he could never say why it happened [COS, p. 333]. That is because, like the rest of us, he didn't know. Why? Because he was talking about something unique, something that nobody understood.

Dumbledore may well have wanted to find out exactly why the effect occurred. But as for the rest of us, we should simply be content to know that it did.

The Verdict

Every single Harry Potter reader has a view on whether Harry is a Horcrux or not, and opinion is split straight down the middle. Not everyone can be right, however, and by the same token it can't be the case that both of these arguments are right.

The most crucial part of the whole discussion centers around why Harry shares Voldemort's powers and how he got his scar. The explanations of how these powers were transferred and the scar created provide solid evidence that Harry is indeed a Horcrux. Voldemort's order that Harry not be killed makes perfect sense in this situation.

The future is clear for Harry, and it was set out in plain and simple terms by Dumbledore. Harry must destroy the four remaining Horcruxes before he can fight Voldemort. If Harry is a Horcrux, he may need to sacrifice himself to destroy the last Horcrux and ensure Voldemort's defeat. Nobody wants to see Harry die. A crack in a ring does not prove that removing a Horcrux from one's body will kill one, however. And so while the path is harder, it does not automatically lead to Harry's death. Perhaps, just in time, he will realize that you don't need to break the object to break the Horcrux. After all, didn't Dumbledore remove the enchantment from the ring while leaving it intact save for a broken stone [HBP, p. 503]?

Harry won't figure it out on his own, though. He'll need some help. When Harry needs assistance of this kind, usually it's Hermione who steps in. She's good at making deductions. She even figured out that when Harry saw visions of Sirius being tortured, they weren't real; they were just a ruse to lure him to the Ministry of Magic [OOTP, p. 734]. However, on this occasion the help will come from someone else.

Step forward, Peter Pettigrew. Wormtail hangs around with the powerful an awful lot, listening an awful lot, and taking in everything he hears—and he's not as dumb as a lot of people make him out to be. Peter's eavesdropping has led him to learn more than a thing or two about his master's Horcruxes, and we know that he is bound to Harry by a life debt [POA, p. 427], which you can find out more about in Chapter 8. Wormtail is a cringing coward, and so what he does will be involuntary; he will be forced to do it by the magic of his debt. But when it comes down to the wire, and Harry is preparing to sacrifice himself to render Voldemort mortal, it will be Peter who will tell him that he doesn't have to die to break the Horcrux. And that is how Wormtail will pay off his debt.

Harry will be left to destroy the Horcrux within him. And when he does, he will be able take on Lord Voldemort, having truly ensured that the Dark Lord is mortal once more.

All in all, it still would be a more pleasant ending (particularly for Harry) if he were not a Horcrux. Unfortunately for him, the balance of evidence says that he is.

Harry or Voldemort: Who Wins?

> *"...Voldemort said that he only killed my mother because she tried to stop him from killing me. But why would he want to kill me in the first place?"* [SS, p. 298]

Until Book 5 came out, we could only speculate. But OOTP answered this question by introducing us to the prophecy:

> *"The one with the power to vanquish the Dark Lord approaches....Born to those who have thrice defied him, born as the seventh month dies...and the Dark Lord will mark him as his equal, but he will have power the Dark Lord knows not...and either must die at the hand of the other for neither can live while the other survives...."* [OOTP, p. 841]

The "one with the power" is Harry, as we explain below. J.K.R. on her website [J.K.R. website] has stressed the importance of this prophecy, and we must understand it if we want to know what is going to happen in Book 7. Here we try to explain exactly what the prophecy is, and what it will mean for Harry in his battle against Lord Voldemort.

True and False Prophecies

First, we need to examine the nature of prophecies. Prophesies may be true or false. True prophecies are made by *Seers*, witches or wizards who are gifted with the power to foretell events. Seers are born, not made, and are exceptionally rare. A prophecy made by a non-Seer is merely a prediction, with no more magic running through it than the Muggle weather forecast.

While Seers can divine the future, the events that they prophesies may not come to pass (as seen with some of Sybill Trelawney's more ridiculous predictions) [HBP, p. 512]. Dumbledore has stressed on many occasions the importance of choice. This means that even the events foretold by a true prophecy can be altered by an individual's deliberate actions. A true prophecy foretells what will come to pass if, and only if, certain courses of action are followed.

A true prophecy cannot be physically destroyed. The tangible record of the prophecy may be destroyed, but the prophecy itself will still exist. When Harry enters the Department of Mysteries, he discovers a room where there are rows and rows of glass spheres that contain a copy of every prophecy ever made [OOTP, pp. 776-80]. These are not the original prophecies themselves, however; they are merely the records. When Harry and his friends smash the spheres [OOTP, p. 804], only the records are erased—not the prophecies themselves.

True prophecies, however, can remain unfulfilled. Dumbledore tells Harry this in so many words:

> *"If Voldemort had never heard of the prophecy, would it have been fulfilled? Would it have meant anything? Of course not! Do you think every prophecy in the Hall of Prophecy has been fulfilled?"* [HBP, p. 510]

So in some cases, a true prophecy can be fulfilled only when someone chooses to fulfill it.

Is the prophecy about Harry and the Dark Lord true? This prophecy was made by Sybill Trelawney, a Seer of dubious qualifications. Her performance as a divination teacher is constantly criticized, particularly by her students and by Professor McGonagall, and Trelawney certainly has a knack for making hilariously off-the-mark predictions [POA, pp. 106-107]. But while her performance as a divination teacher leaves something to be desired, she has a penchant for making her more important prophecies accurately. In *Prisoner of Azkaban,* Trelawney predicts that Peter Pettigrew, the "loyal servant," will rejoin Lord Voldemort, his master [POA, p. 324]. This prophecy is confirmed with the revelation that Pettigrew has allied once again with Voldemort [GOF, p. 7]. Her other important prophecy, of course, is the BIG one she made about the person who will vanquish the Dark Lord [OOTP, p. 842]. This prophecy is set in motion by the birth of Harry and Neville, both born in the seventh month to parents who have thrice defied Voldemort, and the events that it prophesies will ultimately be determined by the choices that Harry and Voldemort make [HBP, p. 512].

What Does the Prophecy Mean?

The only person who heard the entire prophecy was Albus Dumbledore, who was present when Sybill Trelawney made it. One of Voldemort's supporters—later identified as Severus Snape [HBP, p. 545]—was listening at the door, but he only heard the first part of the prophecy:

> *"[Snape] heard only the first part, the part foretelling the birth of a boy in July to parents who had thrice defied Voldemort. Consequently, he could not warn his master that to attack you would be to risk transferring power to you— again marking you as his equal."* [OOTP, p. 843]

Thus, as things stand now, Dumbledore and Harry are the only two people in the world who know the entire text of the prophecy (not even Trelawney knows of the prophecy since she goes unconscious when she makes it) [HBP, p. 427]. This gives Harry an advantage over Voldemort, since Harry understands the full nature of the prophecy and what will come to pass.

The prophecy makes the following points:

1. The one with the power to vanquish Voldemort will be born at the end of July to parents who have escaped Voldemort's grasp three times.
2. Voldemort will identify this person and mark him as his equal.
3. This person will have special powers that Voldemort "knows not."
4. Either this person will kill Voldemort or Voldemort will kill him.

These are broad and ambiguous statements, but that is no accident. On her website, J.K.R. has told us more than once that the prophecy can be interpreted in a number of ways, and that it requires very careful reading. As of the end of HBP, however, we believe that most of the prophecy has come true. Here are our reasons for thinking so.

The first point states that the person who will defeat Voldemort will be born at the end of July to parents who have thrice defied Voldemort. There are two possibilities: Harry, born on July 31 to James and Lily Potter, who defied Voldemort three times, and Neville Longbottom, born on July 30 to parents who also defied Voldemort thrice.

Dumbledore, however, presents evidence which proves that Harry will be the one to vanquish Voldemort. As the second point states, Voldemort will identify and choose his potential destroyer. Voldemort did just this, in Godric's Hollow, after murdering Harry's parents. In doing so, he marked Harry as his equal. The prophecy did not indicate whether it would be Neville or Harry who would defeat Voldemort; it was Voldemort who made that choice:

> *"He chose the boy he thought most likely to be a danger to him," said Dumbledore. "And notice this, Harry. He chose, not the pureblood (which, according to his creed, is the only kind of wizard worth being or knowing), but the half-blood, like himself."* [OOTP, p. 842]

Because Voldemort chose Harry, and marked him with the scar, it is Harry and only Harry who can destroy Voldemort [OOTP, p. 842].

We will discuss the third point, that the chosen one will have special powers that Voldemort "knows not," in more detail shortly (it's too important to gloss over here), but first, let's review the fourth and final point of the prophecy:

> *"… and either must die at the hand of the other for neither can live while the other survives."* [OOTP, p. 841]

Either Harry or Voldemort must die "at the hand of the other." They cannot live alongside each other. So at least one of them is going to die in Book 7.

The Importance of Choice

As Dumbledore explains, however, it is not the prophecy itself that causes this to be true. The prophecy merely reveals a future that *may* come to pass. It is up to the individuals to decide which path they will take. We saw this with Voldemort when he *chose* Harry and not Neville. Harry could choose not to fulfill the prophecy, but because of the murder of his parents, the deaths of Sirius and Dumbledore, and everything else that he has had to go through, Harry will pursue Voldemort until the bitter end. He doesn't have to attempt to kill Voldemort (and Voldemort doesn't have to attempt to kill Harry) simply because the prophecy says so, but they will choose to do so because of the actions that have already been set in motion:

"...the prophecy caused Lord Voldemort to mark you as his equal.*...you are free to choose your way, quite free to turn your back on the prophecy! But Voldemort continues to set store by the prophecy. He will continue to hunt you ...which makes it certain, really, that—"*

"That one of us is going to end up killing the other," said *Harry.* [HBP, p. 512]

For Voldemort, this represents the ultimate irony. The only reason Harry can now face him with any hope of defeating him is because Voldemort overreacted after he heard Snape's incomplete version of the prophecy. As Dumbledore puts it, he "leapt into action" [HBP, p. 510] and marked Harry as his equal. In so doing, he gave Harry powers—the ability to speak Parseltongue, the ability to see his thoughts—that have made Harry's job much easier.

He also intensified Harry's ability to love by murdering those nearest and dearest to Harry. As Dumbledore says to Harry:

"...despite your privileged insight into Voldemort's world.... you have never been seduced by the Dark Arts, never...shown the slightest desire to become one of Voldemort's followers!... You are protected...by your ability to love!...The only protection that can possibly work against the lure of power like Voldemort's!" [HBP, p. 511]

In effect, Voldemort created his own enemy. And that is why the prophecy is important. Not because it predicts the future or tells us what will happen in Book 7, but because it allows the characters to choose their own destinies and change their own paths. Because of this, the fact that Harry has been told the prophecy is more important than the prophecy itself.

Of course, this still leaves us with a burning question. *Which one* will die at the hand of the other—Voldemort or Harry? Is there anyone who doesn't hope that it will be Voldemort? But how can a mere teenager with an incomplete magical education defeat the most powerful Dark wizard of all time? To begin answering this question, let's take a look at a few things that point to the way in which the final battle will go down.

Priori Incantatem

As we learned in the first book of the series, the wand chooses the wizard, rather than the other way around [SS, p. 85]. Ollivander's wand store in Diagon Alley sells wands made of various woods and three known magical cores: dragon heartstring, phoenix feather, and unicorn hair. When Voldemort—then Tom Riddle—went to Ollivander's to buy his wand, he was chosen by a wand with a phoenix feather at the core. Many years later, when Harry goes to the same shop to purchase his wand, he experiments with dozens of wands, none of which seem to work. Eventually Mr. Ollivander develops a hunch and tries one particular wand—a wand with a phoenix feather core. As we all know, that wand chooses Harry and Ollivander explains that the phoenix that produced the tail feather for his wand produced a core for only one other wand—Lord Voldemort's [SS, p. 85]. Thus Harry and Voldemort have what are called "brother wands."

The significance of this fact does not become apparent until Voldemort is reborn in *Goblet of Fire*. What happens then is spectacular. Following his rebirthing, Voldemort gives Harry one last chance to defend himself in a duel. Harry and Voldemort cast spells at the same time, and because they have brother wands, their spells collide and establish a connection:

> *"And then—nothing could have prepared Harry for this—he felt his feet lift from the ground. He and Voldemort were both being raised into the air, their wands still connected by that thread of shimmering golden light."* [GOF, p. 663]

This effect is known as Priori Incantatem, and it has important implications for Book 7. Harry and Voldemort will never be able duel in the final battle; their wands will do the same thing every time they meet. Harry will have to find some other way to defeat the Dark Lord. Will it be a wandless curse? Will Harry disarm Voldemort first? Or will Harry receive a little help from his friends (Snape, perhaps)? Only J.K.R. can answer these questions. But we know one thing for sure: The final battle won't be your typical mano-a-mano (or wando-a-wando) duel; there are going to be some big surprises in store.

Harry's Scar

When the killing curse rebounded on Voldemort the night he murdered the Potters, Harry was transformed into a Horcrux (see Chapter 12), thus establishing a mental connection between the two of them. In *Order of the Phoenix*, we see this connection in action. Whenever Voldemort is feeling particularly emotional, Harry feels a blinding pain in his scar. Images that Voldemort sees are often unintentionally transferred to Harry's brain, such as when Voldemort attacked Mr. Weasley [OOTP, p. 463]. Voldemort becomes aware of this and uses the connection to his advantage by deliberately placing false images of Sirius being tortured in Harry's mind. He does this to inflict pain on Harry and to provoke him into making hasty decisions [OOTP, p. 727]. Professor Snape's attempts to teach Harry Occlumency were designed to prevent this sort of thing from happening, but the lessons fail miserably due to their mutual disdain [OOTP, p. 537].

In *Half-Blood Prince*, Harry no longer feels pain in his scar from Voldemort's emotions, and images are no longer being forced into his brain. From this we may infer that Voldemort is using Occlumency to keep Harry from sharing his emotions and thoughts. Having realized that the connection works both ways, the Dark Lord is feeling vulnerable, so he closes the connection. Might there be a few things Voldemort doesn't want Harry to see? We're not going too far out on a limb by saying: YES, ABSOLUTELY! If Harry is able to hone control of this mental connection in Book 7, he will be able to use this to his advantage, stealing secrets and spying on Voldemort from inside the Dark Lord's own head. This could be a turning point in the battle. Perhaps by gaining enough insight into Voldemort's thoughts, Harry will figure out how to defeat his arch nemesis once and for all.

Love

But even if Harry is able to use his connection with Voldemort to his advantage in Book 7, it doesn't change the fact that Harry is still just a young schoolboy going up against the most evil, powerful, and ruthless wizard in the world. How can he possibly win against these enormous odds, especially with two of his most powerful allies (Sirius and Dumbledore) lying cold in their graves? The answer is simpler than you may think. And it all goes back to where we started: the prophecy. The third part of the prophecy states that the chosen one will have a power that "the Dark Lord knows not." What is this special power? As we learn from Dumbledore in OOTP, it is the power of love:

> "You are protected, in short, by your ability to love!" said
> Dumbledore loudly. "The only protection that can possibly
> work against the lure of power like Voldemort's!" [HBP, p. 511]

But why is love such an important weapon?

We saw how love saved Harry's life once before. It's the only reason Harry is the Boy Who Lived and not just another one of Voldemort's victims [SS, p. 299]. On the night the Dark Lord went into Godric's Hollow to kill Harry, the one thing he overlooked was the power of love. Harry's mother, Lily Potter, was completely self-less that night. When Voldemort told her to step aside so that he could get an open shot at Harry, she refused and was killed in his place. Lily's love was the weapon that saved her son [SS, p. 299].

Dumbledore (and J.K.R.) have frequently stressed the importance of choice. Tom Riddle, who would become Lord Voldemort, grew up in an orphanage where no one loved him [HBP, p. 266]. Harry grew up in the Dursleys' household, where no one loved him, either. The difference is that Tom Riddle chose to seek vengeance against the world that had ignored him, while Harry chose to seek friendship as soon as he got the chance. In other words, Tom Riddle chose hate, while Harry chose love. This choice is what gives Harry an advantage over Voldemort. Harry's heart is full of love, while Voldemort is consumed by hatred. Love is an emotion that Voldemort is incapable of feeling, an emotion that he simply cannot comprehend [OOTP, pp. 843-44].

In order to defeat Voldemort once and for all, Harry will have to call upon his great power to love. But how will Harry use this power to his advantage?

The Blood Connection

In *Goblet of Fire,* Harry tells Dumbledore about the graveyard episode where Voldemort used Harry's blood to regenerate his body:

> *For a fleeting instant, Harry thought he saw a gleam of something like triumph in Dumbledore's eyes.* [GOF, p. 696]

J.K.R. has said that this is "enormously significant" to Book 7 [MuggleNet/TLC interview, 2005]. But why? What exactly does this gleam of triumph mean?

When Dumbledore learns that Harry and Voldemort now have the same blood running through their veins, he realizes that Voldemort has slipped up again, perhaps fatally this time. But how? Why? What does Dumbledore know that we don't?

It all goes back to Lily's sacrifice for Harry when he was a baby. Lily's love protected Harry that night and Voldemort was unable to harm or even touch him. We saw this protective magic work again in SS when Professor Quirrell (possessed by Voldemort) tried to touch Harry and his hands burned and blistered [SS, pp. 294-95]. Since that night at Godric's Hollow, Harry has always been protected by his mother's charm. Voldemort rightly decides that the only way he can overcome this charm and destroy Harry is to mix Harry's blood with his own and acquire the same protection that has kept Harry safe all these years. As Voldemort says during the graveyard scene in GOF:

> "...I tried to kill him. His mother died in the attempt to save him—and unwittingly provided him with a protection I admit I had not foreseen.... I could not touch the boy."
> ... "His mother left upon him the traces of her sacrifice.... This is old magic...I was foolish to overlook it...but no matter. I can touch him now." [GOF, pp. 652-53]

Voldemort is right: He *can* touch Harry now. But he has underestimated one thing, one thing that will ultimately be his undoing. Lily Potter's sacrifice was made out of sheer love, the one emotion that Voldemort hates and fears above all others. And now, the only power that Voldemort fears, the only power that can defeat him, runs through his very veins. And when it comes down to it, in the final showdown, Voldemort will be attacked from the inside as well as from the outside. Lily's love will defeat him once again. And Voldemort will have brought it all upon himself.

The Final Battle

First off, does Harry have what it takes to win? Is it really plausible for a schoolboy to defeat one of the darkest wizards of all time? With the proper strategy, we say yes. Harry has evaded or stopped

Voldemort in Book 1 when he defeats Quirrell [SS, p. 295]; in Book 2, when he manages to stop Tom Riddle from regaining his physical form [COS, p. 322]; and in Book 4, where he duels Voldemort and escapes [GOF, pp. 667-69]. He also holds out against Voldemort at the end of Book 5, although neither one of them gains the upper hand [OOTP, p. 816]. And, of course, he survived Voldemort's killing curse when he was only a baby. In short, Voldemort has never yet managed to get the better of Harry.

How is Harry able to continually defeat or evade Voldemort on each occasion? We say that it all comes down to love. On each occasion, Harry is trying to help others; he is not just trying to save himself. And on each occasion, Voldemort is trying to kill Harry in an attempt to avoid the thing that he fears most: death. As Voldemort himself says:

> *"There is nothing worse than death, Dumbledore!"*
> [OOTP, p. 814]

In his previous battles with Voldemort, Harry has always gotten sucked into the situation. He never initiates the fight. In *Sorcerer's Stone*, Harry is attacked by a Voldemort-possessed Quirrell [SS, p. 294]. *Chamber of Secrets* sees Harry confronted by Tom Riddle—the young Voldemort—at the moment when he is least expecting it [COS, p. 307]. In *Goblet of Fire*, Voldemort lures Harry into the graveyard using a disguised portkey. And in *Order of the Phoenix*, Harry is deceived by a dream and lured to the Department of Mysteries.

We think Book 7 will be different, however. Harry will take the initiative this time. He won't be returning to Hogwarts because the war will keep him too busy, and like any good general, he will have a battle plan to catch Voldemort off guard. So it's essential to the plot that Harry instigates the battle this time around. His first mission will be to destroy the Horcruxes. And then he will go after Voldemort, knowing that he has made the Dark Lord mortal at last.

It is likely that there will be more than one confrontation, and J.K.R. won't be soft about the casualties of war. In other words, expect some old friends to get killed. As we explain in Chapter 14, we think Hagrid, Lupin, Arthur, and Molly are the most at risk. The good news is that you can count on Ron, Hermione, and Ginny making it through. Harry has already lost his parents, his godfather, and an important mentor in Dumbledore. The loss of his best friends would be one cruel blow too many. With his family gone, Harry's friends are what keep him going and enable him to stand up to Voldemort.

When the final conflict comes, Harry will not be alone, but it won't be Ron, or Hermione, or Ginny who will be with him. No, we say it will be Severus Snape (Chapter 10). In Book 7, Snape will finally show his true colors and turn against Voldemort. His help will be vital, as will that of Peter Pettigrew, who will fulfill his life debt to Harry by saving the life of the boy he once tried to have killed (see Chapter 8).

But how will Harry finally defeat Voldemort? We've already established that there can be no one-on-one duel with wands, and it's out of the question for them to physically fight one another. At some point during the final battle, however, there will be a face-to-face confrontation between Harry and the Dark Lord. But Harry's ordeal in destroying the Horcruxes (particularly the one within himself) will have left him too to exhausted to fight. So Voldemort will appear to be poised for an easy victory.

Snape will step forward and turn the tables, however, at just the right (and most dramatic) moment. His aid will be the final turning point in the battle. With Dumbledore gone, Snape is the only remaining wizard with the ability to take down Voldemort. Snape and Harry will make for a worthy final adversary for Voldemort, but it won't be easy. This will be the ultimate battle of the entire series, after all, so J.K.R. is sure to pull out all the stops. Don't be surprised to see some big dramatic twists. There's a good chance that Snape might sacrifice himself to defeat the Dark Lord and save Harry. After all,

Snape has already sacrificed Dumbledore and his reputation for the good of the cause. Why wouldn't he go one step further?

But only J.K.R. knows the specifics of how this final battle will be waged. Rest assured, however, that Harry will come out alive in the end. He will defeat Voldemort. We repeat: Harry *will* defeat Voldemort! He simply has too many tricks up his sleeve and too much love in his heart not to. Good will triumph over evil. Love will win out over hate. And a new reign of peace will flourish in the wizarding world.

What about Everyone Else?

So far we've concentrated on the specific issues that are likely to be most important in Book 7. These are the big questions that everyone wants answered. There is, however, a huge cast of characters in the series, and while they may not all play a part in the final conflict between Harry and Voldemort, they will all end up somewhere when it's over, even if that somewhere is simply dead.

This chapter offers quick and easy insight into what we think will happen to everyone you care about. The characters are listed in alphabetical order. We are talking major characters here, of course—if you're really that worried about what's going to become of Ernie Prang, you'll be better off working it out for yourself.

Sirius Black

(See Chapter 15: Loose Ends.)

Dobby

Dobby is a free elf [GOF, p. 378] who is now happily working at Hogwarts and even getting paid for it. He'll be sad to see Harry go, of course, but after gaining his freedom from the hated Malfoys, he has found a niche in life that suits him just fine. We don't see any reason why he would leave, unless Hogwarts closes. But that probably won't happen. So Dobby will likely stick around the campus kitchens for a long, long time. Maybe he and Winky will even fall in love someday.

The Dursleys

The affairs of the wizarding world have very little effect on the Dursleys—or to put it more accurately, they have very little effect on Vernon and Dudley. Petunia is another matter; she knows far more about magic than she makes out [OOTP, p. 31]. She has formed the habit of pretending to herself that magic-doesn't-exist-and-even-if-it-did-she-knows-nothing-about-it, however. As a result, she has told Vernon nothing whatsoever about the wizarding world. Therefore, Vernon's only real concern is that if Voldemort does turn up, it might make the neighbors talk, and the last thing he wants is to be associated with any of *those* sort of people.

When Harry defeats Voldemort, it will at least remove this possibility, so Vernon will sleep a little easier. Mainly, though, he will be pleased that now Harry has come of age and defeated his enemy, there's no reason why he should ever have to see Harry again.

Dudley will be equally happy—first, because he will never have to be afraid of Harry's wand again, and second, because there won't be any more Dementors to scare him out of his wits [OOTP, p. 16]. J.K.R. has promised that we will discover in Book 7 just why Dudley was so scared of the Dementors in the first place [World Book Day, 2004]. And that will certainly be worth finding out.

Petunia's connection with the wizarding world will be revealed in Book 7, but don't get your hopes up: She's not an important witch in disguise. According to J.K.R.'s website, Petunia is 100-percent Muggle; she can't use magic and she never will. She knows far more than she's currently letting on about the magical world simply because she was around James and Lily when she was younger [SS, p. 33]. In many ways, Petunia will be happier than anyone to see the back of Harry, because as long as he's around, her "respectable housewife" cover could be blown at any moment. With Harry out of the picture, she can settle down at last into the decent Muggle lifestyle that she always wanted, a lifestyle free of wizards and freaks. She seems unable to hide her knowledge of magical matters when it comes to a crisis, however [OOTP, p. 31], and so it's almost certain that more of this will come out in the process. Therefore, her desperate attempt to conceal the wizarding world and her knowledge of it from Vernon will have failed in the end.

Hermione Granger

At the end of Book 6, Hermione and Ron finally showed the first signs of getting together properly [HBP, p. 647]. They will officially become an item in Book 7. They will fight just as much as they always did—probably more—since they always seem to argue the most when they are actually discovering their affection [GOF, p. 432]. They will be happy in their own way, however.

Hermione will be involved in the coming war because she is always so determined to help Harry (who will inevitably be at the very center of the action). Her determination to help her friends is the only thing that could ever possibly distract her from her studies. But even if in Book 7 we see Hermione neglecting to cram in all-nighters to prepare for her NEWTs, we're sure she'll still pass because she is so naturally intelligent. Ron, on the other hand, better bring his books with him wherever Harry's adventures lead them.

Hermione has always been one for studying, but she hasn't given a awful lot of thought to what she'll be doing with her life post-Hogwarts. She did look over a few Careers Advice leaflets in her OWLs year, however [OOTP, p. 656]. Her continued crusade for SPEW (the Society for the Promotion of Elfish Welfare) [GOF, p. 224] points to a career in the field of minority rights or Muggle relations, and indeed the latter was the subject of one of the leaflets that particularly caught her eye. One way or another she's likely to end up working for the Ministry in some capacity, and have a long and successful career there.

Grawp

Bringing Grawp to live in the Forbidden Forest wasn't one of Hagrid's better ideas, ranking alongside his attempts to raise a dragon [SS, p. 233] and his decision to breed Blast-Ended Skrewts [GOF, p. 196]. The best that can be said about it is that despite Firenze's warning that the task was hopeless [OOTP, p. 604], Hagrid has actually succeeded in making Grawp almost acceptable in human society [HBP, p. 643].

Despite this minor triumph, however, Grawp has no major role to play in Book 7. He might liaise with the giants after Voldemort is defeated in an attempt to bring about a bit more harmony between races, as he is the ideal candidate for this job, but that's the extent of it. In the end he'll have to go back to live in the giant community anyway, so this is the best that we can hope for in the sorry saga of Hagrid's attempt to bring his half-brother to live with him.

Rubeus Hagrid

Hagrid has become increasingly marginalized as the series has gone on. He started off as a major character in SS, and he managed to retain that status in COS (in which he was sent to Azkaban for supposedly opening the Chamber of Secrets) and POA (in which he was heavily involved in Buckbeak's trial). Since then, however, he has played little more than a cameo role. Admittedly, he did act as an envoy to the giants [OOTP, pp. 425-33], but that was nothing that Olympe Maxime couldn't have managed on her own. And in HBP, about all he did was get drunk with Horace Slughorn, leading Slughorn to give Harry the memory that he wanted [HBP, pp. 485-90]. Again, this is something that anybody could have done.

There is no direct evidence to suggest that Hagrid is going to have an accident in the final conflict, and any suggestion that he will be one of those to die is pure speculation. However, there can be no doubt that Hagrid's role has become inconsequential; he is now expendable. With so few people now who answer that description, those who do are ripe for the axe. Sadly, it is likely that Hagrid's time is just about up.

Bellatrix Lestrange

(See Chapter 5: Neville's Destiny.)

Luna Lovegood

Luna's direct involvement in the war came to an end with the demise of the D.A. Throughout OOTP, it seemed that she might become a major character in the series, but for the most part she was used as comic relief in HBP. You can expect more of the same in Book 7, although, as we said in Chapter 7, we think there's a good chance that she'll end up with Neville. It's an odd pairing, but it might just work out.

Remus Lupin

Lupin is an interesting character. He was one of the main players in POA, but has played only a minor role in subsequent books. We have precious few clues as to what the future holds for Lupin. The one thing we do know is that he's not going to be killed by Peter Pettigrew and his silver hand [J.K.R. website].

In HBP we are told that Lupin is undertaking a dangerous assignment, working underground in the werewolf community [HBP, p. 334], and that he has started seeing Nymphadora Tonks [HBP, p. 641]. As to the future, we're purely speculating. Like Hagrid, Lupin has become rather dispensable to the plot, and even though we all love him, he's an easy main character to kill off without doing too much damage to the storyline. J.K.R. has said that her husband was disappointed when she told him she'd be killing a character that he liked:

> *You did tell him which ones were for the chop, and apparently he shuddered and said "No, not that one!"*
>
> **J.K.R.:** *He did on one of them, yes.* [Richard and Judy interview, 2006]

Unfortunately, that one might just be Lupin. He's dispensable, he's fighting on the front line, and he's very much at risk.

Lucius Malfoy

Things don't look too good for the Malfoys. Draco's ready for the axe, and as for Lucius, he's pretty much stuck right where he is now: in Azkaban. The Dementors abandoned their posts as prison guards during OOTP, but the Ministry of Magic must have made alternative arrangements, even though we haven't been given any details. After all, most of the Death Eaters were captured following the battle at the Department of Mysteries [OOTP, p. 817], and as of the end of HBP, they're still in Azkaban.

Voldemort would have loved to get his Death Eater army back; if he could have gotten them out, he would have done so by now. The only conclusion that we can draw is that he couldn't get them out. Therefore, Lucius will stay where he is now—locked up in Azkaban—for the whole of Book 7.

Minerva McGonagall

The issue of whether Hogwarts will remain open has been taken to the school governors [HBP, p. 628], but it seems unlikely that they will decide to close down. The war with Voldemort is at hand, and although Dumbledore is gone, Hogwarts is still by far the safest place for the young wizards of Britain to be. Not all families will see it that way, of course, but many will, and so the school will remain open.

Minerva McGonagall will be the new Head. Her fondness for discipline is well known; in the past she has even gone so far as to take 150 points from her own house when she thought it appropriate [SS, p. 244]. Her leadership skills will make her a stern but effective Head; she doesn't have Dumbledore's knowledge or magical power, but she won't make the same mistakes that the overtrustful Dumbledore did, either. It might just be that (whisper it if you dare) she will be an even better Head than he was.

Peter Pettigrew

(See Chapter 8: Life Debts.)

Harry Potter

What is there to say about Harry Potter? He will destroy the Horcruxes; he will defeat Voldemort (if only by the skin of his teeth, and with more than a little help from Severus Snape); and he will end up with the girl. Book 7 is going to be a torrid time for Harry, but all's well that ends well, and he's got a long and happy life with Ginny to look forward to.

As for what career he will pursue, that's very much up in the air. He wants to be an Auror [OOTP, p. 662], and this remains the likeliest bet; but then again, does he really want to work for the Ministry? He has clashed with them often enough to give him second thoughts about this option. The D.A.D.A. job (now uncursed, following

Voldemort's demise) would be a comfy place for him to end up, but unfortunately J.K.R. seems to have put the kibosh on that possibility:

> *We're curious as to whether Harry is going to have a life after Hogwarts, or if maybe Harry might be a Hogwarts teacher?*
>
> ***J.K.R.:*** *Well … I will tell you that…one of Harry's class-mates, though it's not Harry himself, does end up a teacher at Hogwarts.* [WBUR Radio, 1999]

So it seems that a career as an Auror is the most likely path for Harry after all. And even if he does clash with the Ministry, he'll make a great one.

Nymphadora Tonks

Tonks is a skilled Auror and one of Harry's most valuable allies. As things stand at the end of HBP, she is stationed in Hogsmeade to guard Hogwarts [HBP, p. 158]. In Book 7 she will play a role in the wider war, as an Auror and as a member of the Order, but she won't be directly involved in Harry's battle with Voldemort. She will fight bravely and effectively against the forces of evil, but the final install-ment could be very cruel to her: We think that Lupin, her new boyfriend, will be killed since he is fighting on the front line and has become rather dispensable to the plotlines of the series. If this happens, expect Tonks's bubble-gum-pink hair to turn mousy brown for a while as she mourns Lupin's death, but to return to its naturally vibrant hue again once Voldemort is defeated.

Voldemort

What do you *think* is going to happen to Voldemort?

The Weasleys

There are a lot of Weasleys, and it seems very unlikely that all of them will make it out alive. As Molly says:

"Half the f-f-family's in the Order, it'll b-b-be a miracle if we all come through this...." [OOTP, p. 177]

Molly and Arthur

The most worrying thing for the Weasleys is that Voldemort has systematically destroyed Harry's family, and anyone else who has been like family to him. His parents went first, then Sirius, then Dumbledore. Sirius and Dumbledore were father figures, and Molly and Arthur are the closest thing he has to parents now. Unfortunately this puts them right in the firing line, and we doubt they will make it through even the first half of Book 7. Ever since Voldemort returned, Mrs. Weasley has been having dreams about her family being killed [OOTP, p. 176]. Now it seems that her fears may be realized—and that one of the victims will be herself.

Ron

Ron has remained Harry's loyal friend and supporter throughout the series, even when they've had serious disagreements. It would take some powerful magic for anything to change that now, although Ron may be a little more absorbed in his own affairs now that he and Hermione have gotten together. But you can be sure that Ron will be there for Harry when it counts. He'll do his best to ignore Harry's instructions that he leave Harry alone in his fight against Voldemort. Ron's closeness to Harry, and his determination to aid his friend through thick and thin, will mean that he could become a target in Book 7.

But assuming he makes it out alive, we see good things in store for Ron. He'll have Hermione, of course, which will make both of them extremely happy. As for what Ron's career will be, he has probably given this question less thought than anyone in his year. Ron is not the academic type, so don't look for him to become a professor at Hogwarts. A more likely option is that Ron will follow in Harry's footsteps to become an Auror. If he has stuck by Harry's side for this long already, why wouldn't he continue to do so as the pair of friends becomes adults? Of course, becoming an Auror is tough going, so there's always the possibility that Ron won't make it. If he doesn't, expect him to end up on the administrative side of the Ministry, leading the organization back to respectability.

The Brothers

Bill, Charlie, and the twins will probably only have minor roles in Book 7. Bill will marry Fleur, and he and Charlie will both continue to be a part of the Order of the Phoenix. This involvement could place them in the thick of the action, but there are just too many other plotlines for J.K.R. to worry about for her to really concentrate on them. They've been side characters throughout, and that's not likely to change now. As for Fred and George? Unless J.K.R. does the unthinkable, only one destiny could possibly await them: jokes, jokes, and more jokes.

Percy

Percy was last seen storming away from The Burrow, having been pelted with roast parsnips by his siblings [HBP, p. 349]. He has been a jerk for far too long to stop now. He is a staunch Ministry man, a young Fudge in the making, and although in his own way he is just as committed to the fight against Voldemort as his estranged family, this is as far as the similarities go. Still, he's just the sort that the Ministry likes, so he'll end up with a comfortable career there, where it suits him best. If Arthur and Molly are killed, however, this may be just the sort of terrible shock necessary to shake Percy out of his stupidity and lead him back to reconcile with his siblings. Let's hope it doesn't come to that, and that Percy will find his way back to his family on his own. But unfortunately, he's had ample opportunity to make up before, and it hasn't happened yet.

Ginny

Ginny will be determined to help Harry in any way she can because she believes in the cause and because, of course, she's head over heels in love with Harry. Throughout Book 7, she'll be there right

CAMELOT

If you need any more evidence that Harry and Ginny will get together, just look at her full name: Ginevra [J.K.R. website]. It's one of the many variants of Guinevere, who was the wife of King Arthur in English mythology. Harry is clearly the King Arthur figure of the series: both are leaders and the heroes of their respective stories, both are orphans, both were raised in anonymity without any knowledge of their true identity or destiny. Not only that but both where whisked away as babies by a wise old wizard (in Arthur's case it was Merlin, and in Harry's it was Dumbledore) to their new lives with adoptive parents. The parallels between the two are striking, and just like Arthur, Harry will take Guinevere (i.e., Ginny) as his wife.

alongside Ron and Hermione, providing Harry with all the support he needs. In fact, the old Harry/Ron/Hermione threesome is fast becoming a foursome. And if all goes as planned, she will end up with Harry at the end for a happily-ever-after.

The Survival League

J.K.R. has shown throughout the series that she's not afraid to kill off important characters. After all, if Dumbledore was killed, any-body is fair game, even Harry Potter himself. And it seems that with each book, the stakes keep getting raised. So who's going to get the axe this time? Here's what J.K.R. has to say about the subject:

> *The final chapter is hidden away, although it has now changed very slightly. One character got a reprieve, but I have to say two die that I didn't intend to die.* [Richard and Judy interview, 2006]

Notice that she only mentions those she didn't "intend to die." The implication is that there are other characters she *did* intend to die, meaning that, in all likelihood, more than two characters are going to bite the dust in Book 7. So who's it going to be?

Below is a list of all the major characters with their odds of getting the axe in the final book, presented in order from least likely to most likely.

NAME	ODDS	NOTES
Dobby	100/1	Dobby is cute (after a fashion), loveable, and has nothing whatsoever to do with the war against Voldemort. He's practically guaranteed to make it through.
Dudley Dursley	80/1	As a Muggle, Voldemort would hardly even consider Dudley to be human, and therefore he'd never go out of his way to dispose of him. Nasty Dudley is safe.
Minerva McGonagall	80/1	J.K.R. has already played the "death scare" card with McGonagall, when she was hit by four Stupefy spells when she was trying to save Hagrid from Dolores Umbridge's goons [OOTP, p. 723]. Minerva has an important job to do as the new Head of Hogwarts, and J.K.R. isn't about to kill off another Head quite so soon.
Vernon Dursley	60/1	Vernon is pretty much safe from the wizarding war for the same reasons as Dudley: he is a Muggle and therefore of no interest. His chances of dying are slightly higher just on the off-chance that Voldemort might (wrongly) see Vernon as a father figure to Harry and hence remove him like he did with Sirius and Dumbledore. It's very unlikely, though.

NAME	ODDS	NOTES
Petunia Dursley	60/1	Her odds of survival are the same as Vernon, for the same reasons.
Luna Lovegood	60/1	Luna is a bit-part character, used for comic relief. And killing people isn't funny. She's not involved in the war, and thus she's very unlikely to get the axe.
Percy Weasley	50/1	Percy is estranged from his family and therefore totally removed from the Order of the Phoenix, whose members are the good characters most at risk—not that Percy qualifies as a good character any more. Unless Voldemort decided to blow up the entire Ministry, which is very unlikely, Percy will be fine.
Fred Weasley	50/1	Fred isn't involved in the war; he's a businessman now, and there's no reason for him to get involved. Lack of involvement means lack of risk!
George Weasley	50/1	Fred and George come bundled together, so their risks are reasonably the same.
Nymphadora Tonks	25/1	Tonks is perhaps the first character on this list who has any realistic chance of dying. She is an Auror, and hence is fighting against the Dark Lord and his forces. In terms of the storyline, however, her death will achieve nothing, and so she will almost certainly survive.

NAME	ODDS	NOTES
Charlie Weasley	20/1	Charlie is a member of the Order of the Phoenix, but still only a bit-part player, and his odds reflect that. He'll be out there fighting and as such could face the axe, but like Tonks, his death would be irrelevant, and hence is unlikely to happen.
Grawp	15/1	Grawp's main risk is that he won't be accepted back into the giant community when he returns, and they're well-known for being a violent bunch [OOTP, pp. 429-30]. His survival depends on their goodwill, but while they'd kill a Muggle or a wizard who approached them, Grawp will more likely than not be accepted back into the fold.
Bill Weasley	12/1	Bill has already suffered at the hands of Fenrir Greyback, and a natural desire for revenge is likely to lead him towards a larger role than his siblings in the war. Greater involvement means greater risk, and so while Bill probably won't die, it's not out of the question.
Hermione Granger	12/1	J.K.R. isn't afraid to kill off major characters, but this would probably be a step too far. As Harry's close friend, she'll always be a target, which is why she is higher than some on this list. Her death would be a tragedy for both Ron and Harry, however, and after all they've been through, we just can't see J.K.R. doing that to them.

NAME	ODDS	NOTES
Neville Longbottom	10/1	Neville will be going head-to-head with Bellatrix Lestrange, and that's always a dangerous thing to do (as Sirius would vouch for if he was still alive). It is therefore not out of the question for him to lose in this battle. We're predicting victory for him, however, which is why Bellatrix is farther up this list than Neville.
Ron Weasley	10/1	Like Hermione, Ron is at risk because of his links to Harry. His odds are worse than hers because of his connection to Arthur and Molly, who are very much at risk, and frankly because he isn't as bright as Hermione, and therefore less likely to avoid danger. In all probability he'll still make it through, however.
Ginny Weasley	8/1	Even though she has temporarily split up with Harry, Ginny is the most at risk (out of those from Harry's generation) due to her connection to him. If Voldemort realizes he can get to Harry this way then he'll go after her. Luckily for Ginny, Voldemort's attention is unlikely to wander in her direction.
Lucius Malfoy	4/1	If Lucius were on the outside, he'd be a prime candidate to be killed. As it is, he's stuck in Azkaban and thus probably safe. His odds reflect the chances of him getting out, because if he does, he'll almost certainly regret it.

NAME	ODDS	NOTES
Harry Potter	4/1	Harry will inevitably come face to face with Voldemort, and that's a very dangerous thing to do. There are many fans who believe that while Harry will vanquish the Dark Lord, he'll also die himself, and that's a scenario that can't be ruled out. We believe Harry will win his battle without sacrificing himself, however, and so his odds reflect this.
Remus Lupin	3/1	We don't want to see Remus die, but we can't deny that out of all the major characters, he is one of the most expendable. We know some people are going to be killed, and unfortunately Remus is near the front of the line. It's far from a certainty, but it's a distinct possibility.
Severus Snape	2/1	Severus Snape, like Harry, is putting himself in a very dangerous position. He's going to have to attack Voldemort at some stage, and a very angry Voldemort at that, as Snape will have just revealed himself to be a traitor. He'd have been down as a definite death except for J.K.R.'s assertion that someone had been granted a reprieve, and we believe that person is Snape.
Rubeus Hagrid	2/1	Like Lupin, Hagrid hasn't done anything to deserve to die, except to have no strong role left in the story anymore. He's an Order member just like Lupin, and is on the front line. We

NAME	ODDS	NOTES
		believe he is in slightly greater danger than Remus as he hasn't just started going out with a new girlfriend, and so he doesn't even get the sympathy vote.
Arthur Weasley	Even	Arthur and Molly are Harry's parental figures now, and we know what happens to those. It seems very likely that Voldemort will target them and kill them. We'll be very sad to see them go, but that's the way the Dark Lord works.
Molly Weasley	Even	Molly is very much at risk, for the same reasons as Arthur. She'll be very lucky to make it out alive.
Draco Malfoy	1/2	Draco is about to go on the run from the Death Eaters, and there's only ever one conclusion when someone does that. Regulus Black, Igor Karkaroff— we've seen it all before. Draco's days are numbered.
Peter Pettigrew	1/3	Voldemort has always seen Peter as disposable; it was just really a matter of time until Peter annoyed him. Peter fulfilling his life debt to Harry will certainly annoy Voldemort, and so Peter will be disposed of.
Bellatrix Lestrange	1/5	Bellatrix won't be worried in the slightest about the prospect of going head-to-head with Neville Longbottom. She'll just assume she can sweep him aside, but she'll be wrong. Bellatrix's chances of coming out of this duel alive are very slim indeed.

NAME	ODDS	NOTES
Lord Voldemort	1/100	The one thing that virtually every Harry Potter fan agrees on is that Lord Voldemort will die. Maybe Harry will die, too. Maybe Snape will sacrifice himself. Maybe Draco will run away and be tracked down and murdered. There's a lot of maybes, but only one definite. The Harry Potter series is the tale of a fight between good and evil, and evil will not be allowed to win. Voldemort will die, period.

Loose Ends

In the previous chapters, we told you what we think is going to happen in all of the major plot lines of Book 7. There are, however, a number of loose ends still to be tied up. They may not be of critical importance, but many people can still be found in chat rooms arguing over what's going to happen to Winky and Kreacher, or whether there will be any Quidditch matches in Book 7.

Some loose ends are very easily disposed of because J.K.R. has already told us the answers. Is Viktor Krum going to make another appearance? Is Rita Skeeter coming back? The answer to both of these questions is simply yes [World Book Day, 2004; Edinburgh Book Festival, 2004]. Others are worth looking into in a little more detail—and that's exactly what we do here.

Sirius Black

The main question that needs to be answered about Sirius is simple: Is he really dead?

J.K.R. left the details of Sirius's potential death very vague, with the result that theories about him returning have buzzed around like a thousand mosquitoes, even though he didn't appear once in HBP. This is how his death was described:

> *Harry saw Sirius duck Bellatrix's jet of red light: He was laughing at her. "Come on, you can do better than that!" he yelled, his voice echoing around the cavernous room.*
>
> *The second jet of light hit him squarely on the chest.*
> [OOTP, p. 805]

> *It seemed to take Sirius an age to fall. His body curved in a graceful arc as he sank backward through the ragged veil hanging from the arch....* [OOTP, p. 806]

The first issue raised by these quotes is the color of the spell that Bellatrix hit him with. It's implied that the jet is red, which would make it a non-fatal Stunner spell. The color of the second spell is never explicitly stated, however, leaving open the possibility that spell was green, an Avada Kedavra killing curse. But this seems doubtful since people who have been hit by Killing Curses do not fall in graceful arcs—they just crumple to the ground [GOF, p. 15].

The logical conclusion, therefore, is that the light was red and the spell was a Stunner. But if it wasn't the spell that killed Sirius, what did? The only possibility is that the Veil itself caused the death of Sirius.

J.K.R. has given us precious little information about the veil. Remarkably, she has only ever answered one question about it in an interview, and this was a simple inquiry about how old it was [MuggleNet/TLC interview, 2005]. So we only have the information from OOTP to go on.

We know that the veil hangs from a crumbling archway that stands alone in a room in the Department of Mysteries, and that it flutters even though the air in the room is still [OOTP, p. 773].

We know that the archway and veil affect the minds of those who see it. Some, such as Harry and Ginny, are drawn to it. Others, such as Hermione, are disconcerted. Ron, however, is totally unaffected by it [OOTP, p. 774].

We know that some people hear the sound of people whispering behind the veil. Harry and Luna heard these whispers, but Hermione and Ron could not [OOTP, p. 774]. Luna believes that the voices are those of the dead [OOTP, p. 863], and the books have so far given us no reason to suspect that she is wrong.

Finally, we know that falling through the veil must be fatal. And we know this because Sirius Black is definitely dead, and it wasn't the curse that killed him. Remus Lupin and Dumbledore, two wizards with strong understandings of the Dark Arts, fully believe that Sirius is dead.

> *"He can't come back, Harry," said Lupin.* [OOTP, p. 807]

> *"It is* my *fault that Sirius died," said Dumbledore clearly.*
> [OOTP, p. 825]

Sirius's old house-elf, Kreacher, passes on from Sirius's ownership to Harry's, a fact that would be impossible if Sirius were still alive. We see this in the beginning of HBP when Harry gives Kreacher an order, and Kreacher, though unwilling, is forced to obey [HBP, p. 52].

And of course, final and absolute confirmation comes from J.K.R. herself, who has made the issue of Sirius's demise abundantly clear.

> ***J.K.R.:*** *Yeah. Well I had re-written [Sirius's] death, re-written it and that was it. It was definitive. And the person was definitely dead.* [BBC Newsnight, 2003]

But J.K.R.'s very definitive stance on this issue does not mean that Sirius won't play an important role in Book 7. After all, when asked by a fan why she killed Sirius, J.K.R. responded, "I didn't want to do it, but there was a reason. If you think you can forgive me, keep reading. You'll find out." [World Book Day, 2004].

J.K.R. went even further in alluding to Sirius's potential Book 7 return after a fan asked her what form Sirius would appear in, if we were ever to see him again. J.K.R. responded, "I couldn't possibly answer that for fear of incriminating myself!" [World Book Day, 2004]. It seems pretty clear: We're definitely going to be seeing more of Sirius. But how?

The most obvious way he could return is as a ghost, but that path has been closed down. Nearly-Headless Nick confirms that only those who are afraid of death choose to remain as ghosts [OOTP, p. 861]. And Sirius is certainly no scaredy-cat. He spent his life taking wild risks, often just for the fun of it.

Nick's views are confirmed by Moaning Myrtle's account of her own demise, when she says that she returned as a ghost immediately after her death [COS, p. 299]. Sirius has been dead for a year, and if he was going to become a ghost, he would have done so by now.

So if becoming a ghost is out of the picture, how can we expect to see Sirius? Should we expect a message from beyond the grave? An echo from the wand of Bellatrix Lestrange? A memory in a Pensieve? Another question avoided by J.K.R. gives us some more information on the subject.

> **Interviewer:** *Will the two-way mirror Sirius gave to Harry ever show up again?*
>
> **J.K.R.:** *Ooh, good question. There's your answer.* [World Book Day, 2004]

Sirius gives the mirror to Harry so that Harry can be in contact whenever he needs to, but Harry vows not to use it because he doesn't want to compromise Sirius's safety by making him come out of hiding [OOTP, p. 523]. In the end, Harry does try to use it once, shortly after Sirius dies [OOTP, p. 858]. It doesn't work, so he hurls it back into his trunk and breaks it. Harry's mirror can be fixed, however.

And Sirius's mirror? Well, Sirius should have been carrying it when he went through the veil [OOTP, p. 806]. He intended it as a means of communication that he and Harry could use at any time. It wouldn't be much use if he were in the habit of leaving it at home.

This suggests a message from beyond the veil is the most likely way we'll see Sirius again, but it certainly doesn't prove the matter beyond doubt. The return of the second mirror may just come from something as mundane as a search of Grimmauld Place, as we discover that Sirius really did leave it behind after all.

However, whether it is as a memory, an echo, or a message from beyond, it seems unlikely that we've seen the last of Sirius just yet.

Why Are Harry's Eyes So Important?

Almost everybody who meets Harry for the first time comments on how much he looks like his father, but that he has his mother's eyes. This happens when Harry meets Horace Slughorn:

> *"You look very like your father."*
>
> *"Yeah, I've been told," said Harry.*
>
> *"Except for your eyes. You've got—"*
>
> *"My mother's eyes, yeah." Harry had heard it so often he found it a bit wearing.* [HBP, p. 69]

It is no simple coincidence that J.K.R. keeps making references to Harry's looks (and particularly his eyes) in her books. In 1999 she said, "Harry has his father and mother's good looks. But he has his mother's eyes and that's very important in a future book" [Boston Globe, 1999].

No one except J.K.R. knows for sure why having his mother's eyes is so important. But we believe that it has something to do with the battle between Love and Hate raging inside Harry. After all, if Harry *is* a Horcrux (as we hypothesize in Chapter 12), he has been living with Voldemort's hate-filled soul for most of his life. In the process, Harry has become like Voldemort in several ways. He shares Voldemort's ability to speak Parseltongue, and he can also see into the Dark Lord's mind. As we know, Harry looks like his father but, as we learned in COS [p. 317], he also looks like a young Voldemort. Perhaps Harry's looks are attributable solely to his genetics, or perhaps having Voldemort's soul inside him has influenced Harry's looks more than we know. But either way, living with Voldemort's soul would have surely exerted some influence over Harry's development.

And yet, we see that Harry is good and full of love. He wants nothing more than to defeat Voldemort, and he has never been seduced by the Dark Arts. And this is why we think Harry having his mother's eyes is important. His mother sacrificed herself to save Harry, which is the greatest love a mother could give her child. Having her eyes could be a sign that Harry is truly filled with this love and not the hate of the Horcrux that lives inside him.

Will the Mirror of Erised Return?

The Mirror of Erised is one of the most remarkable magical objects in the whole series. It is notable both for its extraordinary ability to show the deepest desire of whoever looks into it, and for the fact that fans are still fascinated by it a full ten years after its first and last appearance in Book 1, when Dumbledore used the mirror to prevent Voldemort from getting his hands on the Sorcerer's Stone [SS, pp. 289-90]. We have seen nothing more of it since then, yet still it crops up during virtually every Q&A session that J.K.R. holds:

> *What would you see in the Mirror of Erised?* [Barnes & Noble chat, 2000]

> *If Harry was to look in the Mirror of Erised at the end of Book 6, what would he see?* [MuggleNet/TLC interview, 2005]

> *What would Hermione see if she looked into the Mirror of Erised?* [New York reading, 2006]

The bad news for Erised fans is that there is no evidence to suggest that it will make an appearance in Book 7. J.K.R. has hinted that many things may appear in the final book, from Sirius's flying motorbike to Viktor Krum, but she has never once mentioned the Mirror. It hasn't appeared in the last five books; it was Dumbledore's idea to use it in the first place, and now he's dead. No point in getting your hopes up for Book 7, fans.

Will Hogwarts Stay Open?

Harry has said in so many words that he will not return to Hogwarts [HBP, p. 650]. And Ron and Hermione have promised to go with him wherever he goes—although it remains to be seen whether Harry will let them. But whether the trio return or not, the death of Dumbledore has cast a huge cloud of doubt over the future of the school, and many of the teachers—including acting Head Minerva McGonagall—believe that it should close. Following an impromptu meeting of the staff, the decision was made to take the matter to the school governors, who will decide whether Hogwarts will close or not [HBP, p. 628].

We believe they will almost certainly decide that the school will stay open. The way we see it, J.K.R. has said so (albeit indirectly):

> *We're curious as to whether Harry is going to have a life after Hogwarts, or if maybe Harry might be a Hogwarts teacher?*
>
> **J.K.R.:** *Well ... I will tell you that one of Harry's classmates, though it's not Harry himself, does end up a teacher at Hogwarts.* [WBUR Radio, 1999]

If one of Harry's classmates is to become a teacher, this must mean that there will be a Hogwarts to go back to. The school may remain closed for a while, but it will definitely be there in the future. One possibility is that it will close for the year covered by Book 7 and reopen after Voldemort is dead. But the school remains the safest place for the young witches and wizards of Britain, even with the Dark Lord making his final bid for glory. It is therefore our view that Hogwarts will be open for business as usual during the final year of the series, even if Harry Potter isn't among the pupils.

Will There Be Quidditch?

There's a simple answer to this one: No. We've seen the last action of the series, and there will be no Quidditch at all in Book 7. J.K.R. has hinted that she'd have dropped Quidditch before now if the readers hadn't been so into it; she says it was becoming more and more difficult to make the games new and exciting. She has now taken the plunge, however, and gotten rid of it once and for all:

> "You know, that was the last Quidditch match. I knew as I wrote it that it was the last time I was going to be doing a Quidditch match. To be honest with you, Quidditch matches have been the bane of my life in the Harry Potter books. They are necessary in that people expect Harry to play Quidditch, but there is a limit to how many ways you can have them play Quidditch together and for something new to happen."
> [MuggleNet/TLC interview, 2005]

The Quidditch season is over!

What Will Happen to the Death Eaters?

Voldemort's army of followers shrank dramatically after his original fall. At the height of the first war, the Death Eaters' numbers were impressive. Lupin says that at that time the Order of the Phoenix was outnumbered 20 to 1 [OOTP, p. 177], and when Alastor Moody shows Harry a photograph of the 1970s version of the Order [OOTP, pp. 173-74], he names 21 different people. This means there must have been at least 400 Death Eaters at this point.

By the time they reconvene in the graveyard at Little Hangleton, however, less than 40 remain:

> *[Harry] was surrounded by Death Eaters, outnumbered by at least thirty to one...* [GOF, p. 660]

This vast fall points to a frenzy of Death Eater killings carried out during and after the first war—killings that were most likely performed in the name of Bartemius Crouch, Sr.'s infamous "Shoot to Kill" policy [GOF, p. 527]. And most of those who aren't dead are now locked away in Azkaban.

The rabble that remains is in disarray, weakened by internal dissent. More often than not, these disputes center on who was loyal to Voldemort after he fell and who abandoned him. Even in battle, the Death Eaters can't hold their mission together without infighting. We see this during the clash at the Department of Mysteries:

> *"DO NOT ATTACK! WE NEED THE PROPHECY!"*
> *"He dared—he dares—" shrieked Bellatrix incoherently.*
> *"—He stands there—filthy half-blood—"*
> *"WAIT UNTIL WE'VE GOT THE PROPHECY!"*
> *bawled Malfoy.* [OOTP, p. 785]

This internal fighting is a sign of weakness, a weakness that comes from Voldemort's rule by fear as he dishes out torture (and even death) to those that displease him. This will keep his followers in line only so far. After all, people will always fight harder for what they believe in than for what they are compelled to do by fear.

For Book 7 we predict a continuance of the theme that has run through the other books in the series. While the virtuous do not always get their reward (see Cedric Diggory, Sirius Black, and Albus Dumbledore), the most evil characters do get their comeuppance. Voldemort will die, Bellatrix will die, Wormtail will die. By the same reasoning, Fenrir Greyback could well die, too.

As for any remaining Death Eaters, they will be captured following Voldemort's final defeat. They will join their colleagues in

Azkaban, and there they will stay. Voldemort will be dead, and that will be the end for his army of Death Eaters.

Will We See More of the House-Elves?

House-elves have enjoyed an extended run throughout the series, always playing a small, but often vital, role in the plot. In COS, Dobby tries to tell Harry about Lucius Malfoy's plan for Tom Riddle's diary [COS, ch. 2], and then does his best to make Harry go home to avoid the coming danger [COS, pp. 176-77]. In GOF, Winky's actions in helping Barty Crouch Jr. ultimately allow him to escape and take Alastor Moody's place at Hogwarts [GOF, pp. 685-89]. Kreacher's treachery in OOTP causes Harry to travel to the Ministry of Magic, and hence leads indirectly to the death of Sirius [OOTP, pp. 829-31]. In HBP, both Kreacher and Dobby follow Malfoy as he tries to find the Death Eaters a route into Hogwarts [HBP, p. 421], and discover that he is using the Room of Requirement to try to mend the vanishing cabinet [HBP, p. 452].

Dobby is a popular character, and it is unlikely that we have seen the last of him, but we expect him to play only a cameo role in the final book. The last time we saw him, he was happily working in the kitchens at Hogwarts, and most of the action in Book 7 will take place away from the school. Winky and Kreacher are also working in the kitchens, so we don't expect to see much of them, either. But as we said in Chapter 9, we believe that the mysterious R.A.B who stole the locket Horcrux was Regulus Black, and that he was assisted by none other than Kreacher. If that's true, Kreacher will have a lot of answering to do come Book 7.

What about Dumbledore's Army?

Harry creates Dumbledore's Army (D.A.) to train his friends in Defense Against the Dark Arts (D.A.D.A.) when Dolores Umbridge forbids the students to practice defensive spells [OOTP, pp. 242-44]. At its peak, the group has 29 members. When Snape takes over teaching the subject, the D.A. is disbanded [HBP, pp. 137-38]. When Harry leaves to accompany Dumbledore to the Horcrux cave later that year, he nevertheless asks Ron and Hermione to recruit any loyal D.A. members they can find to help keep a watch on Draco Malfoy [HBP, p. 552]. By this time, most of the original members have lost interest, and only Neville and Luna answer the call.

In short, the D.A. is no more. Ron, Hermione, and Neville will have important parts to play in Book 7, but they will be motivated by their individual friendships (and in Neville's case, by his desire for revenge), not by their former ties to the D.A. Dumbledore's Army, like Dumbledore himself, is not coming back.

Who Is the Unexpected Magician?

"There is a character who does manage, in desperate circumstances, to do magic quite late in life, but that is very rare in the world I am writing about." [Barnes & Noble interview, 1999]

This hasn't happened yet, so it must be happening in Book 7. But who can the unexpected magician be?

According to J.K.R., it will be an older person who cannot use magic, and it won't be Aunt Petunia:

Aunt Petunia has never performed magic, nor will she ever be able to do so. [J.K.R. website]

So that narrows it down a bit. Let's assume that it's going to be someone we have already met, and someone who has received more than a passing mention. There are only three people who fit this description, one of whom is a Muggle and two of whom are Squibs: Vernon Dursley, Arabella Figg, and Argus Filch.

We can cross Vernon Dursley off the list. He is too far removed from the magical world to engage in such unnatural and shameful behavior, and besides, he wouldn't have a clue how to do it. Of the two Squibs, we would love to see Filch finally manage to get something out of his Kwikspell Course [COS, pp. 127-28]. Regrettably, though, it seems that it's not going to happen because Mrs. Figg is the far more likely candidate. J.K.R. said that the magic for this mysterious person would be used in "desperate circumstances," and only Mrs. Figg, with Order of the Phoenix connections that may well lead her into danger, is likely to be facing anything of this kind. So there you have it: Mrs. Figg will be the unexpected witch.

What Did Dudley See?

> **Amy:** *What did Dudley see when he faced the Dementors in Book 5?*
>
> **J.K.R.:** *Ah, good question! You'll find out!* [World Book Day, 2004]

Dementors drain all of the happiness out of their victims, leaving them with nothing but memories of the worst experiences of their lives [POA, p. 187]. Muggles can feel the effects of their attacks just as wizards do, but they can't *see* them [POA, p. 187]. So a more accurate question would be "What did Dudley *feel* when he faced the Dementors in Book 5?" because, rest assured, Dudley has no magical blood in him.

So what *does* Dudley feel? He seems to have a particularly violent reaction to the attack. He is unable to walk, he starts to be sick, and he can hardly even speak for quite some time afterward [OOTP, pp. 21-26]. He reacts even more strongly than Harry does when he is accosted by a Dementor on the Hogwarts Express [POA, pp. 83-84], and Harry's reaction was by far the worst of all the people in his compartment.

Dudley has been spoiled rotten all his life, and spends most of his time bullying other children, so he has seen very few things that have genuinely distressed him. The one thing that truly frightens him is magic. This is understandable since the first time he encounters magic is when Hagrid plants a pig's tail on his bottom that has to be surgically removed [SS, p. 59]. He still seems traumatized by this incident three years later when the Weasleys suddenly appear in the Dursleys' fireplace:

> *Next moment Dudley came flying into the hall, looking terrified.*
> *"What happened?" said Harry. "What's the matter?"*
> *But Dudley didn't seem able to speak. Hands still*
> *clamped over his buttocks, he waddled as fast as he could into*
> *the kitchen.* [GOF, p. 42]

We suggest that Dudley's violent response to the Dementor attack is simply a reaction to the memory of what Hagrid did to him. It may seem like an overreaction, but in Dudley's pampered life this is probably the worst thing that has ever happened to him. So when the Dementors attack, it's likely that what Dudley feels is the utter helplessness and fear that he felt back at Hut-on-the-Rock.

What Will Happen to the Ministry of Magic?

As things stand, the divisions between the Ministry of Magic and the Order of the Phoenix are as wide as ever. The Ministry, led for most of the series by the incompetent Cornelius Fudge, has bungled nearly every important task it has needed to address. For examples, just look at the way the Ministry refused to acknowledge Voldemort's return for over a year and how it turned the *Daily Prophet* into its own propaganda machine to slander Harry left and right.

Luckily, Scrimgeour, Fudge's replacement, seems like a more intelligent man than Fudge (though that's not saying much!). Dumbledore describes him as being "able, certainly. A more decisive and forceful personality than Cornelius" [HBP, p. 61]. Despite

Dumbledore's modest praise, Scrimgeour's performance thus far leaves something to be desired, having arrested the innocent Stan Shunpike [HBP, p. 221] and refusing to acknowledge Dolores Umbridge's mistreatment of Harry.

If the Ministry is going to move ahead to regain the respect of the wizarding world, it needs to make important changes. The likes of Dolores Umbridge, who is willing to cast Unforgivable Curses in the name of the Ministry [OOTP, p. 746], must be disposed of. The likes of the officious Percy Weasley must be re-educated. The Ministry must move away from the bureaucratic mess that it is now in and become self-accountable. It must exist for the people and not simply to propagate itself.

All of this will require a lot of upheaval, and the big question that remains is whether Scrimgeour is brave enough to take it on. During HBP, he attempted to do it, but only superficially, without really listening to Harry or taking responsibility for the Ministry's previous failures. It is now up to him to swallow his pride and change. We hope that as an intelligent and astute man, Scrimgeour will do this and lead the Ministry to a new dawn of unexpected competence. Of course, if (or when) Harry defeats Voldemort, the Minister's job will be a whole lot easier. Let's just hope that Scrimgeour has the presence of mind to thank Harry and listen to his advice next time.

All the Rest

With Dumbledore gone, who will lead the Order of the Phoenix?

The main candidate for this job would have been Severus Snape, but unfortunately he is rather busy at the moment. In his absence, the only natural leader left in the ranks is Minerva McGonagall. She has the respect of the major players, such as Lupin, Tonks, and Shacklebolt, and so just like at Hogwarts, Minerva will replace Albus at the head of the Order.

Is Bill Weasley a full werewolf?

There's a very simple answer to this one: no! The after-effects of Bill's brush with Greyback are covered in HBP:

> *... in personality he seemed just the same as ever. All that appeared to have changed was that he now had a great liking for very rare steaks.* [HBP, p. 634]

What lies beyond the veil in the Department of Mysteries?

This is best left up to Luna Lovegood to describe.

> *"Oh, come on. You heard them, just beyond the veil, didn't you?"* [OOTP, p. 863]

Luna is referring to her heartfelt belief that she will see her dead mother again, and that the voices behind the veil are those of the dead. Luna has a number of wild flights of fancy and believes in no end of ludicrous things, such as Nargles and Crumple-Horned Snorkacks. On this occasion, however, she might just be right.

Will Dumbledore's portrait be of any use to Harry?

Yes, it will! Portraits retain a certain amount of the knowledge of the person they depict, although far from all of it. J.K.R. explained them as follows:

> *"... The idea is that the previous headmasters and head-mistresses leave behind a faint imprint of themselves. They leave their aura, almost, in the office and they can give some counsel to the present occupant... "* [Edinburgh Book Festival, 2004]

The portraits are honor-bound to give service to the present Headmaster of Hogwarts [OOTP, p. 473], and their service has been very useful on a number of occasions. Harry may not go back to Hogwarts at all during his quest, but if he does, it's only logical that the portrait of Dumbledore will be keen to assist him just as much as it assists Professor McGonagall. As such, Harry will always be able to find a certain amount of help in the Headmistress's study.

Where did Fawkes go at the end of *Half-Blood Prince*?

This one really is a mystery! We know that Fawkes has left the school forever:

> *And he knew, without knowing how he knew it, that the*
> *phoenix had gone, had left Hogwarts for good...* [HBP, p. 632]

We just don't know where he's gone, and there are no clues whatsoever to where he might be!

What did Dumbledore see or experience after he drank the potion in the Horcrux cave?

One thing is for sure—whatever the emerald potion did to Dumbledore was a lot worse than the effect of seeing a Dementor, for example. The potion clearly caused him immense physical pain, but his anguish was mental as well: halfway through drinking it, Dumbledore took to whispering "it's all my fault," and by the end simply bellowed "KILL ME" [HBP, pp. 572-73]. The potion was an invention of Voldemort, and the torments that Dumbledore suffered were of the Dark Lord's design. We can only assume that they were of the most unpleasant kind imaginable.

How and why did Dumbledore have James's invisibility cloak? What is the significance of this?

J.K.R. has said that this question is important:

> *There IS a significant—even crucial—answer.* [J.K.R. website]

According to the note that Dumbledore gave Harry with the cloak, James passed the cloak on *before* his death [SS, p. 202]. It's not hard to figure out why Dumbledore had it. James had just taken his family into hiding in Godric's Hollow, protected by the Fidelius Charm. He couldn't leave the house, but nobody who hadn't been informed by the Secret Keeper could see him as long as he remained inside. So he didn't need the cloak. He was all too aware that his life was in danger, and so it makes perfect sense that he would pass anything useful he could on to Dumbledore, so that the Order of the

Phoenix could make use of it. The cloak most definitely comes into that category.

What is less clear is why this course of events should be so significant. That is something we're just going to have to wait to find out.

What happened to Mr. Ollivander, and since there was no sign of a struggle, whose side is he on?

Mr. Ollivander is a strange man, with pale eyes that blink far too little. He makes the eleven-year-old Harry rather uncomfortable [SS, ch. 5]. Ollivander is also a little too warm towards Voldemort for many people's liking:

> *"After all, He-Who-Must-Not-Be-Named did great things—*
> *terrible, yes, but great."* [SS, p. 85]

His disappearance without a struggle [HBP6] has understandably set tongues wagging a little among Potter fans. Is he working for Voldemort now? The reasons for kidnapping Ollivander are clear enough: He is the premier wand-maker in the country. How better to weaken your enemy than by depriving them of their weapons manufacturer? It may also be the case that Voldemort himself is on the lookout for a new wand, in order to avoid the Priori Incantatem effect that prevented him from killing Harry in the graveyard [GOF, ch. 34].

What will happen to Crabbe and Goyle?

This one has a simple answer—not much! One thing we can be sure of is that they won't say anything. Despite all the menacing looks, intimidating frowns, and threatening knuckle-cracking that they do, J.K.R. has (deliberately, we assume) not had Crabbe and Goyle say a single word in the entire series. Harry and Ron spoke when they were using Polyjuice Potion to imitate them, so we can assume that they are in the habit of talking from time to time. But the real pair haven't uttered a thing in the books to date. Don't expect them to break their silence anytime soon.

Will any Muggle make an appearance in Book 7? How will the Muggle world be affected by the coming battle?

Muggles are likely to be mentioned only in passing. Harry will be with the Dursleys for only the briefest of times [HBP, p. 650], and then he'll leave the Muggle world behind. Voldemort isn't averse to the odd Muggle atrocity or two [HBP, ch. 1] and he might get back to those tricks, but getting slaughtered is about as far as Muggles are going to be involved. They're certainly not going to help defeat the Dark Lord, although at least one Squib—Arabella Figg—is likely to be involved in Order of the Phoenix business somewhere along the way. The most interesting piece of Muggle action will come when we find out more about Aunt Petunia's link to the wizarding world [Edinburgh Book Festival, 2004].

Why was Voldemort prepared to let Lily live at Godric's Hollow?

We believe it was because Snape asked him to. As discussed in Chapter 10, Snape defected from the Death Eaters when he found out whom Voldemort intended to kill based on the half-prophecy that he'd heard. He remained within the ranks to spy on his former master, however, and thus would have been aware of the ongoing plan to track down the Potters. In this situation, it seems more than likely that Snape would ask Voldemort to spare the life of the woman he loved, as it was only Harry that the Dark Lord really needed to kill. Snape has always been a favorite of Voldemort's [HBP, p. 34] and so Voldemort may have agreed.

Did Voldemort go to Godric's Hollow alone the night he tried to kill Harry?

Almost certainly not! J.K.R. has been unusually coy on this issue, and in cases like this, a lack of words says a lot.

> *MA: Was there anyone else present in Godric's Hollow the night Harry's parents were killed?*
>
> *J.K.R.: No comment.* [MuggleNet/TLC interview, 2005]

Logically, Peter Pettigrew for one must have been there. We know this because Voldemort killed Bertha Jorkins with his own wand while still in Albania, where Wormtail tracked him down [GOF, p. 687]. He certainly hadn't been in a position to pick it up himself in the aftermath of Godric's Hollow, and so someone else must have done so. Wormtail had it and took it to Albania, and so it must have been Wormtail who picked it up in the first place.

Rumors abound that Snape was also in attendance that night, but this is harder to justify. He may have been, but any suggestions of this nature are the result of pure speculation and no hard evidence.

What were Lily and James's occupations?

We don't have any information on this at the moment, but what we do have is a promise.

> *J.K.R.: Well, I can't go into too much detail, because you're going to find out in future books. But James inherited plenty of money, so he didn't need a well-paid profession.* [AOL chat, 2000]

We haven't found out up to the end of HBP, so we will find out in Book 7. Given that James inherited a lot of money, and that both he and Lily were members of the Order of the Phoenix at the height of the first war, it seems unlikely that either had a job besides working for the Order full-time.

If Hogwarts remains open in Book 7, who will teach Transfiguration since Professor McGonagall has become Headmistress? Will Slughorn remain to teach potions for a second year even though he said he would only be there for one? And who will be the new D.A.D.A. teacher?

As for replacement Transfiguration professors, there are no obvious candidates among the existing characters, so we predict the introduction of someone totally new. J.K.R. has a history of introducing new characters every time a teaching position needs filling: Lockhart, Lupin, Moody, Umbridge, Slughorn, Grubbly-Plank. So really, your guess is as good as ours.

Professor Slughorn will almost certainly teach potions for a second year. He likes his comforts, and in the war, Hogwarts is about the safest place he'll find to hide out.

If Hogwarts is open during Book 7, they will need a D.A.D.A. teacher for a year. After all, Snape won't exactly be a welcome figure around the Hogwarts campus after killing Dumbledore. Many people expected Lupin to return to fill the position, but J.K.R. shot this theory down cold [J.K.R. website, Rumors section]. If, as we predict, Snape turns out to be good and he doesn't die in Book 7, he will in all likelihood return to his old position when everyone realizes whose side he is truly on. But in the meantime, a brand-new character will have to fill the position.

Is there a connection between Godric's Hollow and Godric Gryffindor?

Yes, there is. J.K.R. has admitted as much:

> *The significance of the place where Harry and his parents lived—the first name...*
>
> *J.K.R.: Godric Gryffindor. Very good, you're a bit good you are, aren't you. I'm impressed.* [cBBC Newsround, 2000]

She's also hinted that there's even more to the Gryffindor connection than that.

> *Is Harry related to Godric Gryffindor?*
>
> *J.K.R.: People are always wondering who Harry might be related to. Maybe he is.* [World Book Day, 2004]

How this ties in with the story is more of a mystery, as these are the only hints we have to go on. Could it have something to do with the fact that Voldemort wanted an object from each of founders of Hogwarts for his Horcruxes? After all, he attempted to murder Harry at Godric's Hollow—perhaps the object he was intending to turn into a Horcrux that night once belonged to Gryffindor. Only Book 7 will tell.

How did Harry's and Neville's parents thrice defy Voldemort?

Again, we'll have to wait until Book 7 to see whether we get an answer to this question. Both Harry's and Neville's parents were in the Order of the Phoenix and would have had plenty of opportunities to battle the Dark Lord during the first war. We think the ways they defied Voldemort will be important, however. Why else would J.K.R. have kept the answer secret for so long?

16

What's Next?

We hope this book has whet your appetite for Book 7. We have tried to cover as many angles as we can, and to answer as many burning questions as we can think of. We encourage you to think about, rethink, prove, or disprove everything that we have said in this book. We always feel that the more information we have, the better position we are in to fully appreciate and understand the implications of the final book.

Book 7 is scheduled for publication in the next few years. We will find out then whether we were right about whether Voldemort will die, whether the trio will survive, and whether Snape is evil or not. We will learn the outcome of the wizarding war and the fate of the characters we have come to love. There will be tears, gasps, and sighs of relief. And then will come the solemn realization that there will be no more release parties to attend, and no more books to look forward to.

What are we going to do then? Will the Harry Potter community cease to exist? Will we stop theorizing? Will we stop discussing? Will we stop arguing? For people who consider the goblet half empty, the Harry Potter phenomenon will cease to exist. They may reread the books occasionally, but there will be no more "What will happen next?" But for us Harry Potter fans, the goblet is always half full. For us, the question "What will happen next?" will mutate and evolve into other questions. Questions such as "What *could* happen next?" or "What would we *like* to happen next?" At MuggleNet.com we like to think that there will still be stones unturned and loose ends left. And as long as we are Harry Potter fans, we will theorize and discuss and argue to our heart's content.

Although the release of Book 7 will mark the end of the literary phenomenon, the internet community will continue to prosper, acting as a user base for Harry Potter fans worldwide. On the internet, fans will continue to discuss the revelations in the final book, fully analyze the series as a whole, and speculate as to what could be happening in the Harry Potter universe *right now*. And we will still have two more movies to look forward to. We can expect them to be as dark and exciting as the movies we have seen so far.

The Harry Potter books have allowed us to accompany J.K. Rowling on her journey, but the journey does not stop when all of the books have been released and read. We can develop our own plots and create our own characters and story lines. As long as we have our imaginations, Harry Potter—and the Harry Potter community—will never die.

However you choose to get your dose of Potter, we're sure that all seven books will remain eternally on your bookshelf. The door to J.K. Rowling's world is permanently open, and we at Muggle Net.com will forever be journeying in, analyzing, discussing, and enjoying the world laid out before us.

We hope you'll still be there with us.